Famous Dave Anderson's

Recipes For Success

Get Fired Up! • Smoke The Competition! • Be Famous!

We Use Only The Highest Quality Premium Ingredients in Our Recipe for Success

Written By:
Famous Dave Anderson
James W. Anderson

www.FamousDaveAnderson.com

Have Famous Dave Anderson or James Anderson Speak to Your Audience!

If you would like more information on having Famous Dave Anderson or James Anderson speak at your next event, or if you would like to attend one of their training seminars, please visit their websites

www.FamousDaveAnderson.com

www.JamesAndersonProductions.com

Famous Dave's Recipes For Success Is The Perfect Gift:

- This is the one book that every parent should buy their graduating senior. They won't need a lifetime to figure out what you learned the hard way!

- If your life seems stuck in neutral, this book will energize you to add the sparks back into your life. Start experiencing life to its fullest now!

- If you have to start your life over, this is the one book that will jump-start your new life. Take Charge of your life now and begin to unleash your greatness!

- If you are a business owner, this is absolutely the one book you should buy every one of your employees. The insights in this book will energize your employees to greater accomplishments!

For information regarding special discounts for bulk purchases, please contact: info@FamousDaveAnderson.com

ISBN 978-1-4507-1399-3

www.FamousDaveAnderson.com

INTRODUCTION

My Dad, Famous Dave, has always been a night owl. He has often said working late at night is when he does his best work. I have always been an early riser, especially as a boy. I usually rose between 5 am and 6 am in the morning. I would creep downstairs and go to the kitchen, get a bowl, some cereal, and a tray (so I wouldn't spill on the floor) and sit and watch the morning cartoons before I had to get ready for school. Some mornings, I would get up and creep down the stairs and smell the powerful aroma of BBQ sauce. I would think, "Uh oh, the kitchen is going to be a mess." And sure enough, it was.

Before Famous Dave's, my Dad was just a man who had a passion for BBQ. Some nights after everyone went to bed, he spent all night creating the perfect sauce, and because I woke up so early in the morning, I was the first person to witness the unbelievable chaos.

There on the stove would be the BIG VAT of his yet-to-be-award-winning championship BBQ sauce. And throughout the kitchen—granted, it was not a big kitchen back then—were all of his supplies, pots, pans, and every spice, seasoning, herb, fruits imaginable… and some not so familiar ingredients that went into his BBQ sauce experiments. Part of me was frustrated because I had to push the mess out of the way to prepare my morning cereal and another part of me was fascinated by everything that went into creating my dad's sauce. There were many interesting bottles of exotic spices, weird looking fruits, and fragrant herbs. Then there were grinding tools, chopping knives, and all sorts of measuring cups. I had a lot of fun just looking at the rows of other bottles of BBQ sauces that he had collected on his many travels to other BBQ joints to get ideas for his own sauce. It was an amazing scene. In a way, I felt like I was in either Thomas Edison's or Dr. Frankenstein's lab. Famous Dave's award winning sauce is a collection of many individual ingredients that, when put together, became a great tasting sauce!

Over the years as I was growing up, I had the firsthand opportunity of living through my Dad's failures and successes. I witnessed him overcoming his battles with drinking and now living a life of sobriety, I lived through both the family's tough times and unbelievable success.

Even though my Dad suffered from Attention Deficit Disorder, he developed an unbelievable drive to learn and has become one of the most passionate students of life and achievement. I believe one of the greatest learning lessons for me is the fact… that if my dad could succeed… so can anybody!

I feel fortunate my Dad wanted nothing but the best education for me, including encouraging me to attend many lectures, seminars, and success boot camps. Together, using the lessons I have learned and the lessons my Dad learned through his many failures and success…we built one of the best leadership and achievement training seminars in the country. We took all of the treasures of achievement, success, and leadership that we learned over the years through my Dad's success in developing one of America's best-known restaurants, Famous Dave's of America, as well as our LifeSkills Center for Business Leadership training, and created this book.

This book is a collection of many great ideas, wisdom, philosophy, tools, tips, and strategies. In many ways, this book reveals our secret sauce recipe for success. We laid out all of the ingredients on the table and now it is up to you to put them together into the big pot. The difference is… the big pot is YOU. You have the opportunity to be like a world-class championship, award winning sauce if you have the proper tools and ingredients. By reading this book, you will be putting the finest ingredients into your head, you will have access to the best tools, and each time you read this book you will be educated, inspired, influenced, and motivated to overcome your obstacles, accomplish your goals, and achieve your dreams.

Here are three key points to think about before you read this book.

1. Now, like any recipe, you must work at it. The more you get to know the ingredients and the tools, the more successful you will be. Make this book a daily read, read ten pages, read one page—whatever it is, make sure you are filling your brain with the ingredients for success.

2. Be patient. Greatness takes time. My Dad's sauce wasn't famous overnight; it took months and years. Yet, if he stopped at any point during that time, the sauce would not be famous and neither would he.

3. Don't make this your only resource for your success. I remember the kitchen being full of other sauces—BBQ, steak, ketchup, etc. My Dad liked to taste other sauces to get a feel for what they did to create his own great sauce. Make sure you are reading other books on personal development and are attending inspiring seminars, trainings, and lectures to hear about what other ingredients are available to add to your own recipe for success.

We are very excited that you have taken the time to invest in yourself by purchasing this recipe book of success. In this book are the best quality ingredients that have been carefully selected and tested over time to create a recipe for success that has proven to work. I want to challenge you to write down your Action Steps after every lesson...do this without fail and by the time you are finished with this book...you will end up with your incredible Recipe for Success!

–**James Anderson,** James Anderson Productions and Co-Founder, LifeSkills Business. www.jamesandersonproductions.com and www.LifeskillsBusiness.com

Famous Dave Anderson's Recipes For Success!

Congratulations!

If you are reading this... I am excited for you because you are about to discover your own recipe for success. Famous Dave's of America, The World's Best Barbeque Joint...featuring America's Best Tasting Ribs has won more first place awards than any other restaurant in history! Over the years, as I have walked through my restaurants many of my customers have asked me how I was able to take a backyard hobby and turn it into one of America's most amazing success stories. In this book, I am "spilling the beans" sharing my own hard earned lessons that have created my Recipe for Success.

My Son and Co-Author, James Anderson

I am also proud to say that my son James has worked side by side with me as we opened the first Famous Dave's and then helped create our incredible personal development training company...The LifeSkills Center For Leadership. At the time of this writing, in a 9-year career, James has trained several thousand people reach break through results in both their professional and personal lives. I am proud to say that James has developed into a very successful entrepreneur and world-class personal development trainer and his insights were invaluable in writing this book.

How To Use This Book

Getting Started: This is not a book to give you ideas! This is an Action Guide for getting more results than you ever dreamed possible. I am challenging you to start writing down your dreams and turning them into meaningful goals that will dramatically change your life. Every day, you MUST absolutely have a list of six things that you MUST get done in order of their priority. If you do this without fail... You Will Unleash Your Greatness! ...and you'll be amazed at the great things YOU WILL start to accomplish.

Most importantly... there are NO excuses. Get rid of all of your excuses about why you haven't succeeded. Next, get rid of all of your blamefulness. If you are brutally honest with yourself you will find that there is no one but yourself to blame for the things that have gone wrong in your life. From now on take full responsibility for yourself. You are 100% totally responsible for EVERYTHING that happens in your life. There are no excuses and you are responsible. This is NOT NEGOTIABLE! If you fail, that is your responsibility. If you succeed, congratulate yourself... you've earned it!

These real life strategies are the lessons that I learned the hard way through believing that my dreams would come true and by working hard. Today, I have made millions, created tens of thousands of jobs, helped others realize their dreams, and have been able to give millions back to helping my community. This book will do the same for you. It will show you how to use your energy to get results. Trying does not count you MUST get results. There are only two things that really matter... The first is your reputation for being excellent at your job and getting results. The next is using your skills and talents to improve the lives of other people. If you can improve the lives of other people... then you have unlocked the treasure chest to unlimited wealth and greatness.

Make sure you thoroughly understand the significance of the first twelve strategies... the rest of the lessons in this book will serve to strengthen and build on the first twelve. We have included Action Steps after each strategy for you to write down at least one thing that you can start to work on immediately. Next, get yourself a good quality notebook that you will write your Action Steps in. This notebook will become your Life's Vision Book and your Life's Plan.

Make a commitment to yourself that you are going to follow through writing down your Action Steps after reading each strategy. But most importantly you must act immediately on the steps that you just wrote down. Here's the key to writing down your Action Steps... never write down your answers like it is something "you're going to try and do." For example: "I am going to be the best rib cook in world. The word "try" is self-defeating. The Secret to Unleashing Your Greatness is writing down your answers for each Action Step in "Affirming Actions" as if you have already achieved the result. For example: "I make many families happy by serving The World's Best Tasting Barbeque Ribs!"

Once you complete this book and you have disciplined yourself to following through on your Action Plans your life will be transformed forever and you will be positioned to unleash your greatness!

May you always be surrounded by good friends and really great barbeque!

Rib-O-Liciously Yours...

"Famous Dave" Anderson, Founder
Famous Dave's of America, Inc.
America's Best Tasting Ribs!

Disclaimer Notice: The opinions and ideas presented in this book do not represent the opinions of Famous Dave's of America, Inc. the company. These opinions and ideas are only representative of David W. Anderson, AKA Famous Dave. This book and/or its ancillary materials is not intended for use as a source of legal or accounting advice.

4

Recipes For Success Ingredient #1:
Anything Is Possible

Take Full Responsibility For Yourself
And Everything Becomes Possible!

Anything is possible the moment YOU MAKE THE DECISION that you are going to take full, 100% responsibility for your own destiny. Your dreams are spiritual seeds of greatness but so many people sabotage their greatness by creating self-defeating limitations in their own head. From now, on start believing that you were put here on this earth to fulfill something great. You are amazing. You are incredible. Don't ever give up on yourself! Everything is possible when you believe Luke 1:37, which says, "All things are possible with God!" Pursue your dreams with all-out passion and unwavering devotion until they are manifested into reality. Become known for making the impossible... possible! No one can make you fail, the same way that no one can be responsible for your success. If it's to be—it's up to me. Anything is possible if you are committed to working your butt off to make your dreams come true!

All dreams come true if we have the courage to pursue them.

~Walt Disney

Take Action Now!

Write down the one thing that you would do if money was no object and there was no risk of failure. Next, write down how this one thing will serve to make the world a better place. What's stopping you from making your dream happen? Write down the steps you would need to overcome the obstacles. Next, write down the six things that you can do right now to get started... NOW go out... do these things, and start making your dreams come true!

Recipes For Success Ingredient #2:
Do The Things That Must Get Done

Successful People Start Everyday Doing
The Things They Don't Want To Do First!

This Is The Major Secret Differentiating Successful People and Unsuccessful People! Successful people do what they don't want to do, consistently day-in and day-out, without fail. Unsuccessful people do whatever it is they want to do. It doesn't matter where you come from or what you've been through... everyone... EVERYONE can become highly successful beyond his or her wildest dreams. Right now, stop whatever you are doing and write down the one thing that, if you did this one thing, it would dramatically transform your life. You must start doing this one thing first! Think about it... "What is the one thing that you know you should be doing that would move you closer to your goals... realizing your dreams... both professionally and in your personal life?" Don't procrastinate any longer. Successful people are decision makers. Make a decision to do what needs to be done. Start right now and do this one thing. Make up your mind that you are going to force yourself to start doing the things that you know you must do! This Is So Important. You Know What Needs To Be Done. No More Excuses. From Now On... Do What You MUST To Do!

> *Do the one thing you don't want to do every day and you will astonish yourself about what you really can do! I have made this my life's pledge: I do what others will not do. Make this your hallmark... and unlimited opportunities will soon be knocking at your door!*
> ~Famous Dave Anderson

Take Action Now!

Write down the one thing that you are not doing but that you know that you should be doing because it will move you closer to your goals, both professionally and personally. Take Action NOW!

Recipes For Success Ingredient #3:
Know How To Prioritize

Every Day Successful People PRIORITIZE
The Things That Must Get Done

The Next Secret About Successful People: They Have Clarity of Vision and Purpose and They Know The Priority Of The Things That Need To Get Done First. You must have a clear vision of what it is you want to achieve. See yourself in your mind as if you have already succeeded and <u>prioritize the things you need to get done everyday in order of their importance.</u> This is critically important: keep a 3 × 5 card in your pocket with your major goal written on top and the three things you must do every day to help drive you closer to your goal. Several times a day, pull out this card to keep you on track. When you are done, check this one thing off your list… AND DO NOT MOVE ON TO THE NEXT THING UNTIL YOU HAVE COMPLETED THE THINGS IN ORDER OF THEIR PRIORITY! Whatever you don't get done… move these things to the next day. Celebrate in your mind throughout the day your vision of success. I call this "My Daily Mini-Celebrations and Revivals." Doing the things that must get done in order of their priority will keep you on track… driving you relentlessly through all challenges and obstacles… to achieve your Vision and Purpose.

> *Winners relentlessly push themselves every moment to do what needs to be done… when they need to get done. Losers do things casually whenever they please and then why they end as up casualties!*
>
> ~Famous Dave Anderson

Take Action Now!

Get a stack of 3 × 5 cards. Write your major goal on top. Next, write the one major thing you must do that will help you move closer to your goals as described in Strategy #4, and then list the top six things you must do each day in order of their importance. Now, get a move on… Take Action NOW!

Recipes For Success Ingredient #4:
Do It Now!

Your Greatness Starts NOW!

The Number Three Greatest Secret of Highly Successful People... They Just Start. You don't always need to know how it will all work out. Don't wait until you have everything figured out. Don't wait until everything's perfect. There is never a better time to start. If you wait until everything is perfect... you'll never get anything done. You will make mistakes... that's OK. Your mistakes may temporarily challenge you... but this will force you to figure things out. This is how you learn. This type of learning is priceless! The Universe favors those who take bold action and attracts resources to you once you have taken massive action towards your goal. Begin. Start Now. A wise businessman once shared this wisdom with his young apprentice... "Act boldly and unseen forces will come to your aid."

JUST DO IT!

~Nike

Take Action Now!

Think about any projects that you know you should do but just can't get started or can't finished. Are these projects critical to your success? ...if they are... make a decision to start now. Put these projects on your list of things that must get done! From this day forward... never hesitate... Start. Just Start.

Recipes For Success Ingredient #5:
Unwavering Faith

Great Faith Unleashes Greatness!

Faith is believing in something you cannot see or understand. All great achievers have been people of deep faith. When you are doing the impossible... the depth of your faith... what you believe... and the power of your prayers... will be the difference between failure and success. Unwavering faith in your dreams and daily prayer... asking for wisdom and strength... is the key to manifesting your dreams into reality. Prayer is the foundation of faith. Faith comes by hearing, Romans 10:17. When you pray unceasing, 1 Thessalonians 5:17... <u>you are repetitiously empowering your mind</u>. Faith is the foundation of belief. Without the power of faith and belief... there is no substance to make your dreams come true. The Bible in Hebrews 11:1 specifically refers to this... "Faith is the substance of things hoped for, the evidence of things not seen."

When you are doing the impossible and you are creating new opportunities... you must have unwavering faith in your dreams to manifest... into reality... something that does not exist. All great societies throughout history have recognized the power of prayer and meditation. Staying focused on your goals throughout the day is the same as praying unceasingly. Know how to pray because "Worry" is also a very powerful form of prayer! You don't want to self-destruct your own vision with a head filled with worry. Your unwavering faith and belief supported by massive action will attract all the resources in God's great Universe to your aid.

> *You cannot expect Million Dollar Answers to 10¢ prayers!*
> ~The Wisdom of The Universe

Take Action Now!
Program your mind for doing the impossible. Every night before you fall asleep, repeat to yourself over and over again: With God All Things Are Possible!

Recipes For Success Ingredient #6:
Break Out of Your Comfort Zone Addiction

Try Something New That Scares
The Heck Out Of You!

Go where you have never gone before and do what you have never done before. You will never find what you are capable of achieving if you don't challenge yourself to move into the unknown. Your greatness is revealed when you attempt the impossible. Quit thinking comfort and security. Comfort should not be your goal... but many people are so addicted to their comfort zones that they get almost sick at the thought of losing the security of their "comfort zone." Force yourself out of your comfort zone. You will never know your true potential until you force yourself beyond what you think is possible. The next time that you are faced with an opportunity that seems beyond you... don't hesitate... go ahead and do it. Thomas Edison said, "If we did all the things we are capable of doing, we would literally astonish ourselves!"

> *The human mind, the human body, and the human spirit... were designed to be challenged to the point of near breakdown... only then can you see that it's possible to go even further! Don't let yourself down by succumbing to a self-limiting mindset of comfort.*
> ~Famous Dave Anderson

Take Action Now!

Identify three ways you have consciously or unconsciously created "comfort zones" in your life and think about how this has held you back. An example of creating a self-defeating comfort zone might be... "I don't get involved with community organizations because I am self-conscious about meeting new people." Write down three Action Steps you can do right now to jumpstart yourself out of these comfort zones. Remember to write down your answers in the affirmative... "I love meeting new people and look forward to joining the local Chamber of Commerce."

Recipes For Success Ingredient #7:
No More Fear

Challenge Yourself To Face Your Fears

You are AMAZING! You were born amazing. Everything about you has been designed by an Almighty God to do the impossible and to achieve greatness. Don't live an unfulfilled life protecting yourself from the things you fear. General Douglas MacArthur said, "There is no security in life, only opportunity." The masses live quiet lives of desperation because they are afraid to face their fears. They fear ridicule and criticism if they fail. These are not good reasons to keep you from doing the things you fear. Overcome your fears by doing things you have never done before. Here's the key lesson: The best security you will ever have... is your ability to consistently transform yourself into something greater.

> *Twenty years from now... you will be more disappointed by the things that you didn't do than by the ones you did do. So throw off the bowlines. Sail away from the safe harbor. Catch the trade winds in your sails. Explore. Dream. Discover!*
>
> ~Mark Twain

Take Action Now!

Write down a list of all of the things that you would like to do but have been afraid to try. Do something little every day to help you overcome your fear. Prioritize the things you fear most that might be necessary that you accomplish to achieve your main goals. Next, go after the things that will help transform you into a fearless person... like speaking in public, parachuting, bungee jumping, white water rafting, ropes challenge courses, and military style physical fitness boot camp! Remember... it's important that you write down your answers in the affirmative... "I love speaking in public and next Tuesday will join The Early Risers Toastmasters Club."

Recipes For Success Ingredient #8:
Embrace Discipline

Embrace Discipline To Turn Your Talents
Or Skills Into World Class Expertise

Daily Disciplines. Your lifestyle is a direct reflection of your daily disciplines. Don't fear discipline. Make discipline your friend! When you are tough on yourself... life will be easy on you. Your dreams will never become reality without discipline. Once you start moving toward achieving your goals... your daily disciplines become your routine systems of success. Discipline is often misunderstood. People generally think discipline confines them and is about restrictions. Actually, discipline gets you doing the things that need to be done... quickly creating accomplishments ...which frees you. Accomplishments get you recognized as a person who gets things done... and this reputation attracts the valuable resources into your life to do the things you want to do! The people without discipline are often held hostage by the consequences of their unrestrained impulses. Without discipline, your goals are nothing more than wishes. The greater you discipline... the greater your creativity. Just think about what you could accomplish if your discipline was as great as your dreams!

> *Discipline is the bridge between goals and accomplishments.*
>
> ~Jim Rohn

Take Action Now!

Write down your top talents or skills that you feel are your greatest strengths. Identify the talents or skills that are needed to help you achieve your dreams. Write down how you will discipline yourself into mastering your talents. You may need to seek coaching, night classes, more lessons, or more practice. See yourself in your mind successfully practicing these skills as you achieve incredible success in your life!

Recipes For Success Ingredient #9:
Start Believing You're Awesome

You Are Amazing, Gifted, and Blessed!

You Have Everything Within You To Succeed Right Now! Many people never get started on the road to success because they believe they don't have what it takes to become successful. They fill their heads with self-imposed limitations... I need a better education... I wish I were smarter... If I was a different race... I never get a break... If I came from a better family with connections. Forget all that stuff. God has blessed you with your own set of unique talents and skills. You have the seeds of greatness within you right now! All you need are the strategies that the rich and the successful have discovered. Just follow the strategies in this book and you will be on your way to realizing incredible success... more than you ever dreamed possible! Here's the key: You have to follow through on the things that must get done every day of your life without fail. Have confidence in your ability and then be tough enough to follow through.

> *Great achievements are accomplished by ordinary people with unwavering determination, extraordinary passion, fueled by a dream of greatness that is unstoppable.*
>
> ~Famous Dave Anderson

Take Action Now!

On a separate piece of paper, NOT in your Vision Book... write down a list of all of the self-imposed limitations you feel have been holding you back. For example: I am afraid to speak in public. Now, in your Vision Book write down a corresponding list of all of the positive opposites. For example: I love speaking in public and people love to hear me share my dreams and aspirations! Next, take your list of self-imposed limitations and in a safe place like a empty coffee can in your backyard... burn this list... while celebrating that you no longer have any limitations and that your weaknesses are now your greatest strengths to helping you achieve your greatness!

Recipes For Success Ingredient #10:
Take ACTION Now!

All-Out Massive *ACTION*

Be a self-starter. Don't wait for things to happen... make things happen! You cannot casually or nonchalantly go about accomplishing your goals... you must be purposeful with great intention. There millions of people out there that are competing against you. Create your own opportunities by out working, out studying, out performing, out giving with every ounce of effort and energy you've got! Stand Up and Stand Out over the masses. Don't ever hold anything back. Give whatever you do 100% of your effort and then reach down and find something deep down and give your effort another push. Walk 25% faster. When you consciously think about walking faster every time you walk... you will develop the habit about thinking about how to improve your productivity in everything you do throughout the day. Be the pace-setter. Work to have others keep up with you. Work until you are spent. In football terminology... leave it all out on the field! Create a reputation for being a person who gets thing done. Be a person of ACTION! You will never regret your hard fought valiant effort. Mark Twain said, "It's not the size of the dog in the fight, it's the size of the fight in the dog!"

> *Most of our obstacles would melt away... if instead of cowering before them... we make up our minds to walk boldly through them!*
> ~Orison Swett Marden

Take Action Now!

Think about every area of your life... how can you get things done quicker? How can you produce a little more each day? When the company or your organization asks for volunteers, be the first. Be a front row-seater type of person. Be the first one at meetings. Just do something a little bit better every day, give a little bit more every day, be just a little bit faster and more productive every day.

Recipes For Success Ingredient #11:
Live To Serve Others

Your Greatness Is A Direct Reflection On Your Ability
To Make A Positive Difference In The Lives Of Others

It's Not About You. Don't Be Full Of Yourself! Live Your Life In Service Of Others. Most people's goals are about what they want. You will achieve greatness if your vision is not focused on what you get... but on how you can better the lives of others. If you are focused on bettering the lives of those in your influence... you will live the life of your dreams made possible by those who you helped to make their lives better. If you are focused on your own betterment... you will live a frustrated life. This is a tough lesson to learn... because most people live their days in pursuit of acquiring. They work to pay off debts from what they've bought for their own enjoyment. When you live your day... "for others" ...there will come a day when the "others" will make it possible for you to have whatever you want beyond your wildest dreams! When the "others" make your dreams come true... that is life's highest reward.

Live your life obsessively devoted to helping others. When you live your life helping others...you will have no time for fear or thinking about what you don't have. Giving of yourself helps you realize how blessed you really are and this is priceless!

~Famous Dave Anderson

Take Action Now!

Think about how your talents and skills can make a positive difference in the lives of other people. How can you bless other people? How can your life, your ideas, your work make this world a better place? How can you live your life "Obsessively Devoted To The Service Of Others?" Answer these questions and you will begin create your own recipe for success!

Recipes For Success Ingredient #12:
Update Your Goals Daily

Reinvent Yourself By Constant Updating of Your Goals

You cannot achieve your greatest dreams being the person you are now. The secret of highly successful people is they rework their goals on a daily basis. The goals you set for yourself yesterday are the goals of somebody less then, hopefully, the person you are now. Which means you need to be constantly setting new goals. Constantly updating your goals is especially more important today in this new accelerating marketplace that is changing so fast; we have to be more alert as to how we keep ourselves current and relevant. Productive goal setting is like exercise. You don't exercise once a year...it is best to exercise daily or at least 3 times a week. Goal setting requires the same commitment. You don't write down your goals once a year and then place them in a drawer and forget about them. You have to work your goals daily. Goals are designed to challenge you into something greater. As you become greater you need bigger more challenging goals. The best goal setting exercise will stretch you to something greater then you are right now. If your goals don't dramatically transform you and challenge you then they are not worthwhile goals. You should be adding something new and exciting to your resume every six months or you are not growing. There's a difference between hopes and goals ... and hope is not a strategy!

> *To understand the heart and mind of a person, look not at what he has already achieved, but at what he aspires to do.*
>
> ~Kahlil Gibran

Take Action Now!
Pull out your goals and update them right now. Keep your goals handy where you can look at them several times a day. Reinforce your goals in your mind. As you accomplish something add a new goal immediately. Keep stretching yourself to something greater. Experience the exhilaration of achieving goals that challenge you to greater heights of accomplishments. You were born to win!

Recipes For Success Ingredient #13:
Follow Your Passion, Follow Your Dreams

Find The One Thing You Love To Do In Life
And Become Excellent At It

Finding Your Life's Higher Purpose. There's a big difference between working to earn a living and living to make a life worth living. Don't spend a lifetime doing something you don't love to do. Understand the difference between "a hobby that you enjoy" and something you "have a knack" for doing and can become excellent at doing. Many people thought that they could take their hobby and make it their life's work, and then failed miserably. Don't make this mistake! Focus on becoming the best you can be at the one thing you are good at doing. Concentrate all of your effort on this one thing. This one thing should totally consume you! It should drive you until you are masterful at achieving excellent results that people will pay you top dollar for.

Usually, at this point, someone says... I want to be successful but I don't know what I want to do in life. Here's how to find your life's calling. First, ask yourself what are you good at... then follow that path. Second, you can always use your best efforts in service to others. Here's the key lesson: whatever you are doing now ...pour your heart and soul into becoming the best at it... even though this may not be what you want to do in life. If you apply yourself with an all-out 110% effort... your "thing in life," that thing you were meant to do, will make itself known to you.

Some people are blessed at an early age with knowing what they are good at and then they spend every waking moment of their life mastering their life's love. Other people, it seems... the Universe wants them to prove themselves before it is ready to make known what they should be doing in life. The point is... play full out every day, giving everything your full attention and your best effort without holding anything back. Be relentless in your pursuit. Here's what I found out when you live every day working your butt off... the people who are very successful will often come to you and help you discover what you are really best at. If

you don't work your butt off and you don't know what you are doing...
guess what? ...you usually end up hanging around other lazy bust-outs
that also don't know which end is up and have no clue!

*Success in anything is about focus and concentration.
When I coached, I'd say to the players, "Yes, I know you
played hard, but that's not good enough. You've got to
stay focused on the task at hand the entire game.*

~Rick Barry

Take Action Now!

What do you love so much that you would do this one thing for free?
What would make you jump out of bed every morning wanting to get to
work? Write this down. Next, write down how your goal in life will
make a positive difference in the world. Making the world a better place
should be your life's higher purpose. Once you understand the
significance of this... the Universe will give you the resources to unleash
your greatness!

Recipes For Success Ingredient #14:
Identify Your Compelling Purpose

Define Your One Compelling Purpose That Will
Drive You Relentlessly Through Any Obstacle

A Compelling Purpose Overcomes Any Excuse. Have one overall major "Compelling Purpose" that gives you the relentless drive to work obsessively, non-stop, to better your life. Your compelling purpose must be so meaningful to you... that there are NO excuses—period! My compelling purpose is driven by the fact that I have experienced the hardships of being bankrupt... I never want to be in that position again, where I cannot feed my family or take good care of them... and that drives me... this is my compelling purpose. Define your compelling purpose and burn it into every cell of your body. Your compelling purpose will give solid meaning to driving you relentlessly toward your goals.

> *Failures have plenty of good excuses...but the successful know there are no good excuses. Never let life's problems become your excuse. Instead, use your compelling purpose to drive you non-stop to achieving your greatest dream.*
>
> ~Famous Dave Anderson

Take Action Now!

In your Vision Book, create a page with pictures of your compelling purpose that will drive you to your greatness. Cement these images in your mind. State with certainty that you will never waiver under pressure and break your promise to your compelling purpose.

Recipes For Success Ingredient #15:
Your Life's Vision

The Universe Cannot Have Any Doubt
About Your Life's Vision

Be a Vision Caster. Stake Your Claim! Learn how to share your dreams. All leaders and successful people know how to inspire, encourage, and get other people to see what is possible. They share their vision. They share their hopes, dreams, and aspirations. They get people believing the impossible is possible. Learning how to speak in public will help you effectively share your vision. Here's a major reason why you must master the art of influencing people... you cannot create successful businesses with negative people... you must be able to inspire them to their own greatness. Learn how to be a vision caster... getting people to believe in a greater vision... and what they cannot see... is one of the greatest assets to achieving your success. When I started Famous Dave's, I told everyone who would listen to me that I was going to build The World's Most Successful Rib Joint featuring America's Best Tasting Ribs! To achieve anything less wasn't even thinkable.

Where there is no vision... people perish.

~King Solomon

Take Action Now!

Prepare a 30-elevator speech that is explicit in detail about your life's greater vision. Share this vision with passion and enthusiasm every time you get asked about your life's plan.

Recipes For Success Ingredient #16:
Speaking in Public

The World Needs To Hear
What You Have To Say

Learn How To Speak In Public. Learning how to speak in public or in front of a group of people is almost non-negotiable, and you must master this to be truly effective in business. To which, most people will say, "I could never speak in front of group... I am not that good!" ...or they say, "I am really a shy, quiet person." I think most people are astounded when I tell them that I am really a shy, quiet person because when they hear me speak, they see a very turned on, passionate, enthusiastic person that loves to inspire people! I used to be so fearful of speaking in public that I was a nervous wreck. It took me years of standing in my basement in front of a mirror, reading books out loud to myself. Then I forced myself to start speaking in front of small groups. I sincerely encourage you to start standing up and letting everyone know who you are... everyone is important and your ideas, your thoughts, your vision, and your solutions need to be heard. You were put on this earth for a reason... now stand up and let it be known! I encourage everyone to find a local Toastmasters group and join it... it's basically free and made up of people just like yourself who want to do something positive for their careers.

> *There are three things to aim at in public speaking: first, to get into your subject, then to get your subject into yourself, and lastly, to get your subject into the hearts of your audience.*

> ~Alexander Gregg

Take Action Now!

Start greeting strangers you meet on the street. Start speaking up at work and sharing your ideas or solutions. Start sharing your thoughts or knowledge by becoming a small group leader at work or at church. Google the Internet to find your local Toastmaster's Club and join.

Recipes For Success Ingredient #17:
Learn How To Sell

Mastering The Art of Selling, Marketing, Promoting Your Ideas, Services, or Products Is Critical To Achieving Your Greatness

Learn How To Sell. One of the greatest skills that I have learned is how to sell. To this, most people say, "I'm not a salesman!" ...or they say, "I don't believe in pressuring someone into buying something." When people say this... they are ignorant about the value of selling. First of all... nothing moves in this world until it is sold. You are a salesman whether you believe it or not. You will always be selling yourself, your ideas, your service, and your time. If you have a great product or services and you don't help people live a better life through them, then you are doing them a great disservice. You will always increase your value once you learn how to sell... no matter what position you hold in your company. My strongest advice is to invest in a three-day course on how to sell... you'll never regret it!

> *If you don't sell, it's not the product that's wrong— it's you!*
>
> ~Estee Lauder

Take Action Now!

Go online and find the best sales seminars you can find. Make sure you attend one within the next six months. Mastering the techniques of professional salesmanship will jumpstart your way to greatness! Next, listen to audio programs on professional selling in your car.

Recipes For Success Ingredient #18:
A "Can Do" Attitude

A Positive "Can Do" Attitude
Will Jumpstart Your Success!

Whether you fail or you succeed is determined by your choice of attitude. Success is a choice, just as failure is a choice. Your circumstances will never determine your success but "The Attitude You Choose" to deal with your circumstances will determine your success or failure. Also, remember this… your past does not define your future. Believe in yourself. Believe you will overcome any obstacle. Believe in your dreams. Work every moment of the day cultivating positive thoughts with a cheerful attitude. Absolutely don't let negative thoughts get into your mind! Don't read negative articles in the newspapers. Don't listen to negative rants on the radio. Don't listen to negative music that gets you down. Don't go to movies that cause you to feel bad. Protect your mind. Protect your attitude. Stay in the positive and you will attract the positive into your life. People are attracted to people who are upbeat, positive, cheerful, and forward looking. Back up your positive attitude with a non-stop, "Let's Get It Done Hard Working" work ethic. At the end of the day… you always have to produce results!

Go confidently in the direction of your dreams. Live the life you have imagined.

~Henry David Thoreau

Take Action Now!

Take inventory of your life and red flag any negative influences that are incongruent with your vision and goals. Ask yourself …does this thing hinder me or help me achieve my goals? If not… work to immediately remove these negative influences from your life.

24

Recipes For Success Ingredient #19:
Get Energized

ENERGY Is Everything!

Live Your Life With Passion and Unbridled Enthusiasm! Whenever I have shared this advice, I often have people tell me… "I am not like that!" …thinking that I am only referring to being a loud mouth! I am not suggesting that you have to be a loudmouth. What I am challenging you on… is the fact that, YES You Must Let The World Know That You Are Passionate About Your Dreams! This is a book about positive life transformation. You are supposed to learn how to start changing your life. Go ahead and be more passionate! You'll be amazed that what you think is outside your comfort level is generally read by others as "charisma." I have found that you cannot achieve any semblance of success without massive passion and over-the-top energy! You need to have unbridled enthusiasm for what you do in life. Live your life full out with passion that burns through every cell of your body! Be a lot more cheerful. Be a lot more loving. Be a lot more caring. Others who cower because they're concerned about "what others think" will want to stifle you… don't even let them influence you. Live your life with over-the-top passion. Your passion will attract others with similar passion and then the magic happens! When a group of highly passionate people gets together… the combined forces can manifest any dream into reality! Don't be a deadbeat. Consciously think about how you can radiate more enthusiasm. Let others catch your spirit! Become a force for good. It's OK to let the world know that you are alive!

> *Sing with passion. Work with laughter. Love with heart.*
> *'Cause that's all that matters in the end!*
>
> ~Kris Kristofferson

Take Action Now!
Keep a ready smile on your face. Be the force that brightens a room. Speak with enthusiasm. Speak with positivity. Think Energy!

Recipes For Success Ingredient #20:
Lifelong Learning

Non-Stop Learning Unleashes Your Greatness

Begin a Life Quest of Learning. Never say… "I know that" …this is actually the first sign of your ignorance! Avoid people who think they know it all. Be Teachable. Be Coachable. Sponge up all that you can learn on how to be successful or becoming the top industry expert in your field. You cannot do what you have never done before unless you strive every day to become a better person with better skills, so you can keep attempting bigger achievements. The average CEO reads four to five books per month. The average person after high school reads only ONE edifying book that will help them grow. This is why 95% of all people are dead broke by the time they die. If you studied for two hours a night for school… don't you think it makes sense to study for two hours every night or even longer for your career? Study every day to become your best. Do your homework to learn from the best. Practice every day to become The Best of The Best! There is no getting around the fact that you have to study, do your homework, and practice, practice, practice to stay on top of your game. Make learning one of your greatest character strengths.

In all thy getting… get understanding.

~Proverbs 4: 7

Take Action Now!

Begin your quest to master your craft. Research what it will take for you to become excellent in your industry. Write down your own program of "Career Mastery." Set aside time… at least two hours each day to study. Begin your Career Mastery with greater intention than your first day of college. Your pursuit of self-learning should be more intense than your effort in college… however, this will be fun because you will be pursing something that is interesting to you and congruent with your life's goals.

Recipes For Success Ingredient #21:
Take Great Notes

Write, Write, Write… Become The
World's Best Note Taker

If You Think It… Ink It! I have never met any successful person who was not a note-taking fanatic. I don't care how smart or proud you are of remembering things… you cannot be a success without taking notes. Get into the habit of taking notes. I keep 3×5 cards in my car, in my briefcase, by my bed, and by my computer. I always have something to write on wherever I am. I am prepared anytime that a brilliant thought of genius pops up in my head and, for me, I have to be ready to capture that profound brilliance! I am amazed at how many people will be in a meeting and they don't take notes. I am also amazed that when people go to seminars, lectures, or keynotes speeches… they don't take notes. If you are listening to someone who is an expert in his or her field… why wouldn't you take notes? I want to learn all that I can and I have to take notes. Successful people take lots of notes… get into the habit of taking good notes. Go online and Google note-taking. There is good information online on how to become a good note taker. You'll never know when your notes will save your neck or your career!

> *Very often, gleams of light come in a few minutes' sleeplessness, in a second perhaps; you must fix them. To entrust them to the relaxed brain is like writing on water; there is every chance that on the morrow there will no slightest trace left of any happening.*
> ~Antonin Sertillanges

Take Action Now!
Start carrying a notepad with a clipboard everywhere you go. Start keeping 3×5 cards in your car for writing down your brilliant thoughts. Every meeting you go to… get into the habit of taking lots of notes. When you are at home, get into the habit of taking notes as you think about your day. Write, Write, Write.

Recipes For Success Ingredient #22:
Sit In The Front Row

Understand The Dynamics Of Being
A Front Row Seater!

NOTE: In my business career, I have come to believe that "Front Row Seaters" are usually only 20% of the total crowd and these people are generally responsible for 80% of the productivity in any business. I have also noticed that even though I am participating in adult meetings, conferences, and seminars, that a good majority of attendees still carry over bad habits from their school days as they strive to sit in the back row seats. While at a glance this may seem totally inconsequential to a business' success... I disagree wholeheartedly! I feel so strongly about this that I only want to hire "Front Row Seaters!" ...and here's why.

Front Row Seaters signal to the world that they are Showing UP, Standing UP, and Ready To Take On The World! The students who sit in the front rows will be tomorrow's leaders driving the marketplace, leaders in their communities, and the ones who step up to make the world a better place. Front Row Seaters are eager, they are ambitious, and they have an above-average drive to make the best out of their learning opportunities. They have a relentless drive to be front and center where all the action takes place. Being a Front Row Seater means you have to come early... you have to put some effort and energy into scrambling for the highly prized front row seats. There is thought and some strategy necessary for getting the best seat possible.

Being where the teacher can see you means that you need to be fully prepared because you might be called on. Sitting as close to the instructor also shows respect for his or her knowledge and efforts to teach you. Being a Front Row Seater also means that you need to take good care of yourself because you are conscious of making a good impression. Sitting in the front row means that you are confident with a healthy, strong self-esteem, as you are sitting in front of all the other students, subject to their critical eye as they notice everything you do.

By the way, being in the front rows is also a good reason to be a very good note taker... the instructor, teacher, or seminar leader notices easily the ambitious note-takers.

Your industriousness in taking notes will be thought about when leadership opportunities are discussed. Here's a good reason why you want to be noticed by your instructor: Everyone needs letters of recommendation for getting into a school of higher learning or for getting your dream job. From now on, make it a point to be a Front Row Seater! "Scrambling to be front and center" will be a leadership character trait that will be your ticket to greatness!

The Demise Of The Back Row Seater

Back Row Seaters signal to the world that they really don't care. Back Row Seaters... do you realize that not only are you condemning your future but you are condemning your children's future by where you sit? When you sit in the back row, you are establishing a pattern for life. You squash any ambition you have by settling for the leftover seats. Where else in life do you settle for the leftovers? If you are a backrow seater... just look at the people that are in the front rows as they will most likely be your bosses!

It takes no effort to get a back seat. You can come in late. You sit in the back where you will not be noticed. You have a good chance of avoiding being called on so you can get by with not being fully prepared for class. Sitting in the back row shows that you have no respect for the teacher.

You can be sloppy in appearance because no one will notice you in the back row. Creating a great future for yourself is not in your plans... as you rather sit in the back row with your other jackass friends and goof off. It is a well known fact that you will become just like the people you associate with. Unsuccessful people unknowingly take on the behaviors of the people they hang around but here's the important lesson: you don't get challenged to grow. When the class is asked to team up for a project... the backrow losers team up with other deadbeats... and the collaboration and idea generation is lackluster and substandard.

Back Row Seaters usually end up wondering how come the rewards of life pass them by. They get passed over for raises, promotions, and prime assignments that can lead to career-changing opportunities. Ask yourself… Where else does this "Back Row Seater mentality" show up in my life and how has this held me back? Don't let your back row seating casualness turn you into one of life's casualties!

> *Sitting in the back rows of a classroom establishes a pattern for life. You get used to taking a back seat to others ahead of you. Don't get used to the leftovers of life. Be a front row seater, always be first and get a jump start on life!*
> ~Dr. Richard St. Germaine, University of Wisconsin

Take Action Now!

Any class, meeting, or seminar that you go to… get there first and become a Front Row Seater. Take good notes. Ask questions. And volunteer to give answers. Stand up when giving an answer.

Recipes For Success Ingredient #23:
Become A Powerful Question Asker

Look Smart By Asking Dumb Questions…
And It's Really Alright To Ask Dumb Questions!!!

Most people go through life wishing they had asked the question to find something out. In my own life, I remained dumb for a long time because I was afraid to ask a question… because I didn't want everyone to think that I didn't know anything. Have you ever noticed that it's the smart people who are willing to ask questions? Don't ever let your concerns about what other people may think of you affect you… go ahead, stand up, and ask for clarification or better understanding. Have you ever noticed a child when he wants something… the child keeps asking over and over again… children never give up. If you are going to be successful… you need to ask about things you don't know about… go ahead and ask. Always remember, the only dumb question is the one you didn't ask!

All that's different about me is that I still ask the questions most people stopped asking at age five.
~Albert Einstein

Take Action Now!
Ask yourself, "Are there any burning questions that I have that I haven't stepped up and asked?" Make it a point to ask your questions. Get things clarified. Just start asking… "I really didn't understand this and I would like this clarified!" Start asking more questions. Ask. Just Ask!

Recipes For Success Ingredient #24:
There's A Best Way To Ask

Learn "How To ASK"

There Is A Successful Way To ASK: Ask For The Things You Want And Ask With The Expectation Of Receiving It. Most people ask for things never believing that they will get them. Much of success is believing that the Universe stands ready to give you resources if you are doing things for the right reasons, especially if your ambition is to make the world a better place. God teaches you to ask with the belief that you are already in the process of receiving what you are asking for... and who are you to argue with God? So ask for the order. Ask for the sale. Ask for that opportunity. Ask with all of the belief that you will receive what you asked for. Never give up believing. Here's the key lesson: The things you need to accomplish, your goals, will not fall out of the sky and into your lap. You have to ask for the opportunity. You have to ask, "How To Help." You have to ask for resources. You have to ask for help. You have to ask to get paid. Start asking with confidence. Much of your success and your greatness will be depend on how effective you are in asking the right questions.

> *And in all things you ask for in prayer, believing, you will receive.*
> ~Matthew 21: 22

Take Action Now!

From now on... when you ask for something... always ask with the expectation of receiving what you asked for. If at first you don't get what you asked for... keep asking. Never take the first NO as the end of the inquiry. Regroup. Think things through and ask again. Most questions never get answered until the seventh time you ask. Don't ever give up on something that you need to ask for. Your initiative to keep asking is a direct reflection of your character, perseverance, and belief in your dreams.

Recipes For Success Ingredient #25:
Success University

Success Needs To Be Studied Just Like
Any Other Field of Endeavor

Success 101. Did you ever take a course called Success 101 in school? If you never studied "Success" …how do you expect to become successful? You must study success… Success 101 courses include: Financial Literacy, How To Buy Real Estate, How To Build An Investment Portfolio, How To Become An Inspiring Leader, How To Speak In Public, etc. Start a Success Library in your home. "How to achieve success in your life" and "How to achieve greatness" will be a LIFELONG pursuit. The size of a person's home library is a direct reflection of his or her success. The key to success is a daily discipline of learning, going to seminars, lectures, mentoring, continued education, reading every day, and listening to audio tapes in your car. Your learning initiatives must be undertaken with the sole purpose of dramatically transforming you into something greater and better.

> *When I was a boy of fourteen, my father was so ignorant I could hardly stand to have the old man around. But when I got to be twenty-one, I was astonished at how much the old man had learned in seven years!*
> ~Mark Twain

Take Action Now!

Set aside a specific area in your home and start your own Success Library. This Success Library should house your Vision Book, positive inspiring books on leadership, management, creativity, management, and biographies on successful leaders. Your Success Library should also hold your audio books, trophies you have won, certificates of excellence, and any reward or recognition that you are proud to have achieved. Put up positive, inspiring posters of great quotes wherever you can… on your mirror, on your refrigerator, at work… surround yourself with positive, edifying good stuff!

Recipes For Success Ingredient #26:
Coaches, Teachers And Mentors

All Successful People Hire Coaches
To Hold Them Accountable

Embrace the strategy of hiring mentors, teachers, and coaches to take you to the next level. You cannot accomplish your dreams being the person you are right now. One of most destructive things you can do to sabotage your success is believing that you can go it alone. You need someone who will hold you accountable, push yourself outside of your comfort zones, and correct things that need to be corrected. Even the most successful people and champions need coaches to push them "even farther" than they thought possible. A mentor, teacher, or a coach will cut your learning curve in half and help keep you from making serious mistakes that could ruin your career.

Learn from the top experts in your field. You cannot transform yourself with yesterday's teachers. In school, there's a good reason why at every grade level up you get a new teacher. If you want to keep striving to the next level... you need to keep seeking expertise from the top experts in your field. The greater your desire to seek the best wisdom will cost you something. Here's a very important lesson: The greatest lessons you'll ever learn will always come at your greatest expense. The more you have to give up, sacrifice, or lose... the more your desire to achieve your greatest dream will be tested. Be prepared to invest in your future. Don't think twice about investing into yourself... it's the best investment you'll ever make!

Personally, I have a voice coach, a speaking coach, a public relations coach, a marketing mentor, a cooking on TV coach, and several food scientist mentors for product development. I will pay my speaking coach over $20,000 this year, including all expenses. My voice coach runs $500 for a half hour. My "How To Cook On TV For Publicity" coach is $10,000 for a three-day session... but this is why I excel at being a nationally recognized public figure for Famous Dave's, The World's Greatest Rib Joint! The media knows that if they book me for an event or a national TV segment, that I have proven to deliver a great over-the-top media piece for them, and I get invited back over and over again. As a result, I have been on Oprah, Regis and Kathy Lee, CNBC's The Big Idea with Donny Deutsch (four times!), The Food Network, The Travel Channel, The Discovery Channel, Fox Morning Show, NBC, CBS, ABC, PBS, NPR, and over 300 radio stations nationwide.

Even top professional sports athletes like mixed martial arts fighters in the UFC will have strength coaches, boxing coaches, wrestling coaches, ju-jitsu coaches, kick-boxing coaches, nutrition coaches, and public relations coaches. The other day I was watching a World Series of Poker Tournament, and the TV Poker Analyst was commenting on how top poker players all have coaches …a coach for poker strategy, a coach for tournament play, and a coach for how to read body language.

The message is clear… if you are going to succeed at a professional level in any field of endeavor… you need to be coached professionally and held accountable. Set aside a certain amount of your savings to reinvest into hiring the best coaching available to jumpstart your career.

> *Better than a thousand days of diligent study is one day with a great teacher.*
> ~Japanese Wisdom

Take Action Now!

Identify areas in your life where you might need an outside mentor, teacher, or coach. In every industry, industry magazines have sections in which top professionals advertise their consulting services. Invest in your career. Invest in yourself.

Recipes For Success Ingredient #27:
University On Wheels

Turn Your Car Into Your University On Wheels!

Dashboard University. Make your car your "University on Wheels." Listen to audio books in your car. This has been a huge life changer for me... for the last 30 years, I have listened to inspiring messages in my car. Never listen to tunes until you have first listened to something uplifting, motivating, and positive that will help you succeed in achieving your goals. Go to any bookstore and look in their audio books section for audio books on Self Improvement, Inspiration, Leadership, and Management. All bookstores carry biographies on audio books... study great leaders and hear their remarkable stories of how they overcame incredible adversities to achieve great success. Listening to positive, motivating audio books will make a huge difference in your life! It has been said... if you listen to audio books in your car... just during the time that you spend driving around... in three years the knowledge that you gain will be the equivalent of a college education!

> *If you think education is expensive... you should try ignorance!*
> ~Derek Bok, President, Harvard University

Take Action Now!
Go to your local bookstore and check out the audio book section, and pick out something inspiring and edifying. Or go online and search out inspiring leaders, motivational speakers, and management gurus and buy their audio products. The next time you get into your car, listen to an inspiring audio lesson before you listen to the radio.

Recipes For Success Ingredient #28:
iPod Academy

Non-Stop Inspiration Whenever And Wherever!

iPOD Academy. Download MP3 files of positive, inspiring, uplifting audio books. The idea is similar to your University on Wheels. Whenever you have a chance… take motivational expert Zig Ziglar's advice to put The Pure, The Positive, The Clean into your mind. With all the negative stuff on the radio, on TV, and in print… take control of what goes into your mind. Learn good stuff every chance you get!

> *I never stop studying. There's always lots to learn. When you stop learning, that's about the end of you.*
> ~John Morton Finney

Take Action Now!

Make sure that you have great instructional downloads on your iPod or mp3 player. Listen to inspiring, uplifting speeches from the world's best teachers while working out, doing your chores, or while flying or traveling.

Recipes For Success Ingredient #29:
Master Your Craft

Personal Research and Development

Create Your Own Personal R & D Department. Jim Rohn, one the nation's best-known business philosophers, said, "Work hard on your job and you'll earn a living. Work hard on yourself and you'll earn a fortune!" Begin a Personal Research and Development quest to learn everything about your craft or line of work. Make it your goal to have not just a job but to become a world-class expert, a professional, the best in your industry. Learn the company's systems of success. What do you need to know to master your craft and be a leader in your industry? Here's the key: Don't wait for your company to train you… make this your personal daily discipline. One hour of study every day within one year will make you one of the best in your company. Two hours of study every day for a year will propel you to being one of the best in your industry. Within three years, you will become one of the best in the world! Lifelong learning is essential to any lasting success. Invest into your own future.

> *If you employed study, thinking, and planning time daily,*
> *you could develop and use the power that change the*
> *course of your destiny.*
> ~W. Clement Stone

Take Action Now!
Identify one new job skill that you would like to master and begin a nightly study.

Recipes For Success Ingredient #30:
First Impressions Are Based On Your Appearance

You Never Get A Second Chance On First Impressions

Stand Out From The Masses! 55% of how we taken in communication is through body language! Your appearance is part of that! This statistic is critical to all first impressions. How you dress, groom and present yourself is critically important to your success. Next, 38% of first impressions are based on your tone of voice and how you say the words. Only 7% of first impressions are based on the actual words, this is according to a research study conducted by the University of California, Los Angeles. Your words are important, but if your appearance is poor you'll never be heard.

Dress up to go up! Cultivate the habit of taking care of your appearance. Keep your appearance neat and clean. How you hold yourself, your body language, your cheerful smiles and your positive spirit should be immediately noticeable. Work hard to create a positive image of yourself. Never dress for the job you have, always dress for the job you want. A great posture, big smile, pressed clothes, groomed hair, and good smell topped with an uplifting positive talk... will create an aura of brilliance about you. The aura of positive spirit is called "charisma;" this is what makes you stand out from the masses. When you dress sharp everyone in the room will take notice of you. When you dress casually, you blend in and don't stand out. Don't let casualness turn you into one of life's casualties. Give yourself every advantage you can... Look Sharp!

You can't do deals in dirty heels!
~Uncommon Wisdom From A Shoeshine

Take Action Now!

Before you leave the house, look in the mirror and ask yourself, Do I look sharp? Do I look like the type of person that everyone would say...now there goes someone who looks like they are on top of the world! Remember, you never get a second chance to buy back your first impressions. Make all your first impressions your best!

Recipes For Success Ingredient #31:
Help Others Grow

Make Yourself Invaluable To The Marketplace By Helping Others Succeed First

Attentive devotion to helping others develop into the best that you can be… is your best opportunity to create the highest demand for your services. Quit going to work thinking about how you can earn more money. Start thinking about how you can grow your company by helping your team become the best that they can be. Your greatness is really a direct reflection of your ability to put the needs of others first. Once you have learned that it's all about sharing your expertise to help others develop their skills… you will also have figured out that the best payback… is the fact you are now in high demand. You have become invaluable. People who can help others grow into their own greatness become invaluable. Once people cannot do without your ideas, products, and services… you will be able to attract the people who can afford to pay you big dollars! The big dollars only happen when people search you out.

> *The secret to becoming invaluable and becoming in high demand is always giving more than what is expected. To give more… you have to become more. Never quit studying how to become the best …so you can teach what you know… helping others which creates a multiplier effect of your greatness.*
>
> ~Famous Dave Anderson

Take Action Now!
Throughout your day, figure out how you can be more helpful to the people you work with. How can you use your expertise to help them strive to the next level? Next, consciously think about how you can be of greater service to your customers. Be more attentive to their needs. Share your helpful ideas with your clients. Let the people in your influence know that you were thinking of them!

Recipes For Success Ingredient #32:
All Jobs Are Gold!

Treat Every Job As Your Dream Job
And Your Dream Job Will Find You!

Here's one of the secrets to success... every job, no matter how small, is extremely important. More importantly, your attitude about doing even the most menial of jobs reveals how you think about other people who do this job and your readiness for leadership positions. We all find ourselves working at jobs that we don't particularly like but the most successful people do these jobs anyway because they need to get done. I remember one of the first businesses that I owned, and I instructed a new employee that the restroom needed to be cleaned. Without any hesitation or questioning whether cleaning the bathroom was in his job description... this young employee went right to work and did such an outstanding job that your first impression was that you could eat off this floor! I immediately knew this young man had a good upbringing, a great work ethic, and I sincerely believed that he would be a great leader someday. When you treat every job, big or small, like it is your golden opportunity... this is the quickest way to having your dream job find you!

> *If you expect the best, you will be the best. Learn to use one of the most powerful laws in this world; change your mental habits to belief instead of disbelief. Learn to expect, not to doubt. In so doing, you bring everything into the realm of possibility.*
>
> ~Norman Vincent Peale

Take Action Now!

Consciously develop the mindset the from now on that you will do any job that needs to get done with excellence. You will develop a reputation for being the one person that everyone can count on to get things done.

Recipes For Success Ingredient #33:
Developing Your Intellectual Capital

Immerse Yourself Into Your Industry
Develop Your Own Intellectual Capital

Today, knowing "just how to do your job" is not enough... your ambition should be to acquire everything you can to learn about your industry. What you know about your craft and your industry is called Intellectual Capital. What you know about your industry is different than just knowing how to do your job or mastering your craft. Intellectual Capital is when you start mastering all of the details of your industry, and your intellectual ideas or contributions start affecting the whole industry. Your number one goal should be to know who the leaders are in your company and your industry... study them and learn from them.

You need to gain Intellectual Capital or "complete detailed information" about your best customers, your top competitors, the best manufacturers of your supplies, the best vendors who sell your products, and how things are shipped and distributed. The key to Intellectual Capital is to know "How to get things done within your industry." Here's a list of things that you should do to start developing your own specialized knowledge...

Join trade associations where you can develop close relationships with the right industry leaders: company presidents, respected industry entrepreneurs, VPs of marketing, advertising, public relations, industry attorneys, industry banks, accountants, financial advisors, and insurance agents, that specialize just in your industry. These people have a wealth of knowledge regarding what's happening, trends, new innovations or threatening government regulations.

Subscribe to your industry's trade associations and trade publications.

Attend industry conferences and conventions and make sure you attend as many breakout sessions as you can. If your company does not have the budget to send you… go on your own and look at this as an investment in your career. The more the movers and shakers in your industry see you around at industry events, the more you will be regarded as being vital to your industry.

If you have ideas, or have discovered a best practice… share it with your industry and submit an article to your trade association's newsletter or magazine. Pretty soon you will be regarded as an industry expert and will start to be asked to participate on conference panels. Then your value to the marketplace will go through the roof!

> *Skill is fine, and genius is splendid, but the right contacts are more valuable than either.*
>
> ~Sir Archibald McIndoe

Take Action Now!

See if your company has any trade association magazines around and start studying these magazines for things to learn, networking opportunities, conferences, and trade conventions. Get involved! Start developing your Intellectual Capital about your industry.

Recipes For Success Ingredient #34:
Networking

Become A Networking Powerhouse

To become a Networking Powerhouse is as simple as greeting everyone you meet. Learn their names. Treat them like they were the only person on earth that matters to you. When you do this... they will go out of their way to tell the world about you. Be the one who organizes sending birthday cards or arranges to get the cake. Offer to take your supervisors out to lunch. Show up at all after work gatherings and stay later to help clean up. If there are any company-sponsored associations or charities, make sure you get involved. Most of all... never burn bridges! You never know when this person might be in a position to influence your destiny or when you may have to sell something to this person. Unlimited opportunities or the lack of opportunities will be limited only by the size of your address book. The effectiveness of these contacts will be determined by how often you are in contact with these people. Send them articles that might interest them, birthday cards, Christmas or Holiday cards. Invite them to lunch and get to know them. One more key thing... when you introduce someone... be their biggest raving fan. Not only does your introduction say something about yourself... but you also have an opportunity to create a future for the person you are introducing. You never know when the person you are introducing may be introduced to a future employer, a future client, or a future spouse!

> *It's not who you know but what these people know about you and what you know about them... especially if they know that you know!*
>
> ~Famous Dave Anderson

Take Action Now!

Make it a point to get involved with your company's functions and charities, and volunteer to help organize. Start collecting business cards and staying in touch with the movers and shakers in your industry.

Recipes For Success Ingredient #35:
Be A Fan Of Your Company

Be The BIGGEST Raving Loyal Ambassador
For Your Company!

Embody the brand as if you were the founder. Be grateful that your company gave you an opportunity for work. Know everything you can about your company and enthusiastically use your company's products. Be excited when telling your friends where you work and encourage them to buy your company's products. Never bad-mouth the boss and never cut down the company that feeds you, no matter how tough you may think things are. Be your company's biggest raving loyal ambassador. You may think you are doing this for your company... but the real secret is... being The Biggest Raving Loyal Ambassador For Your Company is probably one of the best things you can do for your own reputation in the marketplace and your career!

> *I have never bought from "a company." Bricks and mortar, the plant, the organization doesn't mean much to me. What matters to me is the personal relationship that I have with the person representing the company's products or services that can make me happy.*
> ~Famous Dave Anderson

Take Action Now!
Learn everything you can about your company. Use its products and know how they can make the world a better place. Tell all of your friends about how great your company is and how grateful you are to be employed there!

Recipes For Success Ingredient #36:
Handwritten Notes

Make Handwritten Note Cards Your Calling Card

Write someone today! In this day of digital communication, old-fashioned, handwritten cards are almost extinct. If you want to stand out from the masses, get into the habit of sending specially selected cards or your own specially printed monogrammed card with handwritten notes to key people in your life. You can't put up digital message on your desk or bulletin board. I always respect the time someone takes to hand write a note on a card. When I get cards with manufactured, mass-produced name signatures... I think these people were "too busy" to properly acknowledge me... and I think, "why bother?" Thank people with handwritten cards.

> *I look forward to getting letters. I am especially impressed when someone has actually figured out how to use a real ink pen to write me a personal note. When I see that someone has actually signed their name, then I am ready to vote for them, buy something from them, or even lend them money! (just joking!) There's something magical about a name in real ink on paper in today's digital world!!!*
>
> ~Famous Dave Anderson

Take Action Now!
If you feel the need to thank someone or recognize him or her for some reason... immediately send him or her a handwritten card! This simple strategy will payoff in dividends throughout your career.

Recipes For Success Ingredient #37:
Live A Life Worthy Of High Standards

Set High Standards For Yourself

Your reputation and your career are worthy of the time and effort it takes to create high standards for yourself. You cannot better the lives of others with average performance. Hold yourself to higher standards and hold your associates to high standards. One of the best examples I know of setting the bar high and holding himself to a higher standard was three-time World Champion basketball great Michael Jordan. Michael played full out even in practice, like it was a championship final game. And he expected his teammates to play with the same intensity… if they didn't, Michael was in their faces! Make sure you hold yourself to the highest standards and walk the talk. Areas of high standards may include: integrity, honesty, organization, cleanliness, being on time, dress standards, your language, effort, and a job well done. Stay true to your standards and you will attract the right people into your life.

Famous Dave's is about having the highest standards in the industry. I want to make my standards so high that my colleagues have to challenge themselves to get better. You will never have to apologize for having high standards. Yes, its difficult to work with me… but that's OK… I want the people with low standards to go work somewhere else!

~Famous Dave Anderson

Take Action Now!

List out some areas of high standards or values that are important to you and put these into your life's Vision Book. Think about other areas that you can work on and make it your goal to turn these into your vital life standards that will define your character.

Recipes For Success Ingredient #38:
Stand Up For Your Principals

Stand Up For The Things You Believe In!

The most important thing in your life is to stand up for the things you believe in! We are living in a world where people are more concerned about being politically correct and worried about what other people think than they are about standing up for their own values. Stand up for the things you believe in as long as they are morally and ethically right. No matter how unpopular your view may be, sometimes you need to follow your heart. I am not embarrassed to say… "That God changed my life!" We are living in a country that was founded on the principles of faith… and today, it is almost politically incorrect to say that we worship an almighty living God. I don't agree with that one bit… there would be no Famous Dave's if God did not change my life. You must be able to stand up and tell the world your dreams and your aspirations with conviction and heart. The people hearing you must believe you and they must trust you. The question everyone has to ask themselves is… "What kind of legacy are you leaving? How will people remember you?"

> *I feel that there would be no greater honor than when*
> *my time has come and gone… that people would say…*
> *"There went a God fearing husband to his wife, there*
> *went a God fearing father to his children, and there went*
> *a God fearing leader in his community.*
> ~Famous Dave Anderson

Take Action Now!
Make it a point to stand fast and stand up for the things you believe in, especially if they can make the world a better place. Standing up for what you believe in is a critical ingredient to unleashing your greatness!

Recipes For Success Ingredient #39:
Your Work Ethic

Develop A Great Work Ethic

Make it your goal to have folks say... "There goes the hardest working person I know!" Look forward to going to work. Enjoy your work. Work harder than anyone else. Be willing to work longer hours than anyone else. Be known as the hardest worker in your company. Be a self-starter. Stay busy. Be the pace setter. Push yourself out of your comfort zones. Don't get complacent. A 40-hour work week is only subsistence. Forty hours will only let you squeak by... all success is only achieved by putting in your time. Success comes from the time you invest in before and after your eight-hour day. Never consider that the company owes you for this extra time... always think of this extra time as an investment in your career and your reputation. You don't become exhausted by what you do... you get exhausted by what you haven't done. A job well done is exhilarating and creates a great sense of accomplishment. Make your family proud of you by creating an exciting, rewarding work life. Take great pride in your work. Set an example for everyone else!

> *Worthwhile success is impossible in a 40-hour work week.*
>
> ~Clarence Birdseye

Take Action Now!
Let it be known that you are willing to work extra hours. Be willing to work weekends and on holidays. Be the first to step up to take on problem jobs or jobs that no one else wants to do. Help others succeed at their jobs.

Recipes For Success Ingredient #40:
Readiness From The Get Go

You Better Get Up Running!

"Every morning in the forest, a deer wakes up. It knows it must run faster than the fastest wolf or it will be eaten. Every morning a wolf wakes up. It knows it must outrun the slowest deer or it will starve to death. It doesn't matter whether you are a deer or a wolf... when the sun comes up, you'd better be running."

~Native American Wisdom

Readiness. Start every day like it was your first day of work or the first day of business. No matter whether you've been in business for over 20 years or you've been on the same job for 20 years... start every day like it was your first day on the job. Treat every customer like he or she just walked into your place of business. Be extra nice to everyone. Be prepared before you start work. Prepare yourself the night before to make the most out of the next day. Do your homework. Be opportunistic. Be alert. Be observant. Be attentive. Be willing. Be ready to jump! When needed, don't mope around and look like you need to be wound up to get going... jump and get things moving! Be the first to step up when things need to get done. Be the one person everyone can count on!

The secret of success in life is for a man to be ready for his opportunity when it comes.

~Benjamin Disraeli

Take Action Now!

Every night before you go to bed, make sure you are ready for the next day. Prepare your 3 × 5 goals card. The next day, wake up running and ready to unleash your greatness!

Recipes For Success Ingredient #41:
The Value Of Sacrifice

Understand The Value of Delayed Gratification

Sacrifice or Delayed Gratification. Success and achievement require sacrifice of your personal impulses. Successful people control their desires and personal impulses. The failures in life let their impulsive desires control them. Look at it this way… what you sacrifice is an investment in a better life. And really, you only sacrifice the desires of your impulses. Success requires that you do the things that must get done when they need to get done. There are two forms of sacrifice: Sacrifice of instant personal gratification to stay the journey to become something even greater… and the sacrifice to make someone else's life better. Don't let personal pleasures or impulses keep you from the things that must get done for you to accomplish your goals. Make this your motto: I do what others will not do… so that some day I will have what others will not have!

> *Seize every opportunity, no matter how small, to give your life away in service. Whatever it is that you want to do in life… make the primary motivation of your effort something or somebody other than your desire for gratification or reward. The irony here is that your personal rewards will multiply when you're focused on giving rather than receiving.*
>
> ~Dr. Wayne Dyer

Take Action Now!
You know exactly what personal impulsive desires you have in your life and how these hinder your success. Make up your mind to control these desires now. Take charge of your life and you are getting closer to achieving great success!

Recipes For Success Ingredient #42:
No Short Cuts

There Is No Getting Rich Quick

All Success Requires Tenacity To Stick With Something Until You Reach Your Goals. <u>There are no shortcuts in life.</u> It's not easy in the beginning… but you must stay the course. You must persevere. You can't scam the system and think that you can get something for nothing. The people whose main goal is something for nothing almost always end up with nothing. You have to learn to earn. You have to study. You have to work. You have to put in the time. It is estimated to take 10,000 hours to get really good at something and to become a world-class expert. When you look for shortcuts, you lose learning about the ins and outs of your business. The only way to shortcut your learning curve is to apprentice or learn from someone already highly successful. Make perseverance and tenacity your character strengths. Stay the course. Start now to master your craft so you'll never have to look back with regret.

> *Let me tell you the secret that has led me to my goal. My strength lies solely in my tenacity.*
>
> ~Louis Pasteur

Take Action Now!

Run from anyone who tells you that he or she can make you a pile of money overnight. Know that anything worthwhile takes time, learning, and hard work. There is no substitute for hard work. Stay the course. Stay true to your vision.

Recipes For Success Ingredient #43:
You Must Get Results

Be Competent At Getting Results

Always Finish Your Job And Do It Well. Many people want to make people feel good but are afraid to hold people accountable for getting results. It isn't about feeling good... it's about getting results. In Little League, "playing the game" is important... once you are an adult... you have to get results. Many people talk a good game but have nothing to show for their efforts. You need to produce results. You need to be highly productive. There is no coasting or living life in neutral. Live every moment of your day becoming more productive than the day before. Here's the simple lesson: if you want more... you have to become more than you were the day before and you must produce more than you produced the day before. Just don't be busy... be great at getting results. It's all about RESULTS! No one ever remembers the person who lived their life "trying."

> *A racehorse that consistently runs just a second faster than another horse... is worth millions of dollars more. Be willing to give that extra effort that separates the winner from the one in second place.*
>
> ~H. Jackson Brown, Jr.

Take Action Now!

Make sure you know what results are expected of you. Know how the job you are doing is directly responsible for producing profits. Strive to be a little bit more productive every day. Always give more than expected and soon you will be discovering one of the greatest secret ingredients to your own success!

Recipes For Success Ingredient #44:
Little Things Matter Big Time!

Pay Attention To The Details

Some Say... The Devil's In The Details. I Say... God's In The Details. It All Matters. Everything, no matter how small... is important to your success. You cannot go through life flying by the seat of your pants! Pay attention to the little things that the masses ignore and you will become the one who stands out. Know what you are dealing with. Learn how to ask questions for everything that you don't understand. Take time to read the small print. Learn how to read financial statements. The Wisdom of The Universe says, "Anything big or small that is not watched or managed will deteriorate to the lowest level tolerated." There are problems hidden in every nook and cranny that need to be exposed. It's OK to be nosey. What don't you know about that's critical to your success? What haven't you looked at lately in detail? Develop the reputation for being one who pays attention to the details. Mastering the little things will create the big opportunities. Success in life is not often found in big chunks of achievement but in doing the mundane little things consistently correct... with excellence... over and over again... day in and day out.

> *Success is the sum of small efforts, repeated day in and day out.*
>
> ~ Robert Collier

Take Action Now!

Never underestimate the importance of understanding every detail. The details are critical to your success. Write down the key components of what makes your business successful and then master these things. Be the one who digs into the details when others have a tendency to skim over things. Mastering the details will help you discover how simple the recipe for success can be with the right ingredients!

Recipes For Success Ingredient #45:
Everyone Is Accountable

Success Requires Measurement And Accountability

Anything Significant Worth Doing Requires Measurement. To measure and be held accountable requires good organization. Organize your projects with the intention of measurability. The Wisdom of The Universe says, "Anything that is measured and watched... improves." If you want the responsibility, be willing to accept being held accountable. There are many people who want more responsibility but then they do everything to keep from being held accountable.

Inspect what you expect!
~ Wisdom of The Universe

Take Action Now!

If you want the responsibility, you have to accept being held accountable. Know the measurements by which you are being held accountable. Know every day if you are succeeding or failing. Know if you are going backwards or forwards. Are you making progress? Are you on target? When you know on a daily basis that you are always consistently moving forward... then you have discovered the keys to the kingdom!

Recipes For Success Ingredient #46:
Your Word Is Gold

Your Word Is Your Bond And Your Reputation

Your Word Is Sacred. It represents everything you stand for... don't ever compromise your values and your integrity. Your commitments are gold. Your promise is never to be broken. It's all about Integrity. Your word and your integrity are your reputation. Once you violate your promises... you immediately lose your reputation. It is very hard to regain the trust of others. Don't ever lose this trust. Keep your word no matter what happens. Your reputation is everything!

Your words are powerful. What you write, what you speak, you become. Choose your words carefully. Then can become weapons or they can create beauty. Your words are powerful angels. Your words can make a difference. Use your words to create magic.
~James Hillman

Take Action Now!
Never compromise your values or your word. Keep your word!

Recipes For Success Ingredient #47:
Your Values

Live A Life Of Integrity

Be A Person Of High Values. Don't ever believe that it's cool to be a person of loose morals or anything goes. You will attract similar people into your life... is that really what you want? Will these people help you achieve your highest dreams or aspirations? Your reputation is everything... never lose it... never compromise your values. Once you violate people's trust... you immediately destroy your reputation. It's hard to earn back people's trust and rebuild your reputation. Live a life of integrity and high values. Be a person of great influence that helps create goodness in others.

> *Character may be manifested in the great moments, but*
> *it is made in the small ones.*
>
> ~Phillips Brooks

Take Action Now!
Stick to your values. If something seems fishy to you... don't do it!

Recipes For Success Ingredient #48: Watch What You Sign!

Get Things In Writing And Know What You Are Signing!

Don't Take Anything For Granted… Know What You Are Getting Yourself Into. As much as I am an advocate of trusting people… you need to get things in writing. Just as importantly, know every detail of what you are signing. Don't be afraid of saying… "Let's go over this one more time, I don't know if I fully understand everything."

> *Trust everyone but get things in writing. People mean well but when it comes time to stand on the firing line to get shot… they would rather it be you. I have learned this lesson the hard way so many times that I have often felt like I had "Sucker" stamped on my forehead…therefore I feel well qualified to give this advice. Absolutely know what you are signing!*
> ~Famous Dave Anderson

Take Action Now!
Don't ever sign anything without getting a copy first and having someone you trust go over every detail with you. Let somebody else with "fresh eyes" take a look at what you are signing. If you don't like the feel of things… hold off and sleep on it. Don't ever sign anything unless you are absolutely comfortable with what you are signing.

Recipes For Success Ingredient #49:
Give Your Career A Running Jumpstart

The Two-Year Challenge To
Jumpstarting Your Career

Take Two Years And Totally Devote Them To Complete Focus On Achieving Your Dreams. While you are young and have the physical and mental capacity... this is when you want to give your career an all-out effort. When you went to college... you were totally devoted and made many sacrifices. Why not be totally devoted with the same intensity for your career? If you were committed to studying hour upon hour every day including weekends to make the grade for college... isn't it even more important to study with the same intensity for your career? If you were willing to totally devote four years to college... why not totally devote two years to mastering your career? This is about sacrifice and hard choices that most people will not make.

During these two years, you will not watch TV or see movies or read the newspapers. You will not listen to the radio in your car until you have listened to a positive and inspiring audio book. Everything you read will be devoted to learning a new skill. Every moment of your day will be devoted to achieving your goal. This is why it's important to have a Compelling Purpose that fuels your drive. Your daily moment-by-moment mantra will be... "I do what others will not do!" I do what others will not do... so someday I can do what others cannot do. You will be focused on Mastering Your Craft and Achieving Your Life's Dream.

As hard as this may seem... you'll be grateful for the personal discipline it took for you to set this great foundation for your life. You'll be light years ahead of the masses. The hard work you put into these two years to master your life's work will be the best investment into your career that will pay huge dividends for the rest of your life!

This Two Year Challenge of Total Devotion To You Achieving Excellence In Your Craft... will be one of the most difficult things you have ever done in your life. But at the end of these two years... you will be well on your way to achieving incredible success in your life. Complete dedication is what separates the few successful ones from the masses.

~Famous Dave Anderson

Take Action Now!

Make a commitment to your future, set yourself up for success, and develop yourself to master your craft. Take the Two-Year Challenge. Give yourself the best start in life possible.

Recipes For Success Ingredient #50:
Watch Your Friends

You Will Become Like The People
You Associate With

Watch Who You Hang With! Your friends, neighbors, and relatives can sometimes be your biggest reasons why you can't succeed. Get all of your toxic relationships out of your life. Look around you... do the people you are hanging around with... represent your values? Will these people help you achieve your greatest dreams? Here's the scary thing to consider... you will become like the friends you hang around with! Sometimes you have to practice "nonattachment" ...and you need to move on so you can stay true to your own dreams. If you have plans for your life... don't let people who have no plans keep you from achieving your dreams.

> *Keep away from people who try to belittle your ambitions. Small people always do that, but the really great make you feel that you, too, can become great!*
> ~Mark Twain

Take Action Now!

Take a good look at the people you associate with... will these people help you achieve your life's greatest dreams? Make a decision and challenge yourself to get involved with people who can help you grow into your potential. Get involved with your local school. Join the local Chamber of Commerce. Join a community organization or your local church. Get involved with other people who are committed to making your community a better place to live. When you help your community become stronger... you are contributing the right ingredients for success in your neighborhood!

Recipes For Success Ingredient #51:
Don't Pay Attention To The Critics

Don't Listen To The Naysayers!

Your Dreams And Aspirations Are Precious. Your Mind Is A Treasure Chest Of Greatness... Don't Let Little People With Little Thoughts Rob You Of Your Dreams! This is very important: Keep your own counsel. Follow your heart. Don't ever let other people's negativity overcome your dreams. People will find every reason for why something can't be done. Don't listen to them. Here's an important thing to remember: Often, the biggest negative critics are the people who don't have our best interests at heart, so don't even let them influence your attitude. When things are tough... stay focused on finding ways to overcome your challenges. Always stay optimistic about your achieving your dreams. Stand up... Stand Out From The Masses... that never achieve anything in their lives. Stay focused on achieving your greatest dreams!

Follow the path of the unsafe, independent thinker. Expose your ideas to the dangers of controversy. Speak your mind and fear less the label of "crackpot" than the stigma of conformity. And on issues that seem important to you, stand up and be counted at any cost!
~Thomas J. Watson

Take Action Now!
Counter every negative saying with a positive, energizing, thought... reinforcing your dreams, vision, and goals. Your beliefs are more important than anything anyone else can say... overcome all negativity by unleashing your positive greatness on the world!

Recipes For Success Ingredient #52:
Join Groups That Challenge You

As Challenging As It May Be…
Position Yourself In Groups Of People
Who Will Challenge You To Learn

Surround Yourself With People You Can Learn From. Find friends who challenge you to become better than you are. Hire people who are better than you. Get involved with groups that share your personal vision for growth and achievement. You will become like the people you associate with… that should either challenge you or scare you. When you find yourself knowing more than the people around you… then its time to find some more challenging friends! (don't abandon your friends, just find some new challenging friends)… or, better yet… bring them along and challenge them to grow with you! One of the most amazing things that I have found… is that when I endured the first feelings of being uncomfortable about joining a new group… I eventually discovered my newfound friends to be refreshing and uplifting.

Really successful men are pushed up, not pulled up.
~Thomas J. Watson

Take Action Now!

Find one group where everyone is striving to reach a higher level of accomplishment and join that group. A few ideas: Toastmasters, a physical fitness course, a book club, a cooking class, a neighborhood investment club, a new language course, a sales course, or a night course to get a higher degree.

Recipes For Success Ingredient #53:
Energize For Results

ENERGY IS EVERYTHING!

Your Success Will Be Determined By The Energetic Passion Of The People In Your Organization. While job skills and execution are vital... so is energy! If your execution skills are at an eight in terms of level of competency but you feel your energy is at a seven... 8 × 7 = 56, which means you are running at almost half capacity! Now, if you can up your energy to a level nine and your competency is still at an eight... you are now at 72. Here's the lesson: If your organization can operate at higher levels of competency and higher levels of energy... not only will you be more productive but you will also attract high level performers who will want to join your energizing organization. There are so many benefits for upping your energy levels! While execution is so vitally important in the building phase, you can overcome brief learning periods with an energetic positive spirit. ENERGY is so important... don't even think of investing in your business unless everyone on your team is as passionate about your product or service as you. If your passionate burning desire to succeed is at a level 10... make sure your team members share the same level of passion or they will drag you down and you will fail. Be energizing with everyone you meet. If you don't give energy... you won't receive energy... that is the way the Universe works.

> *Don't shy away from the term "love." Do you in fact L-O-V-E your project? Measure it on a Love Scale: 1= Turnoff; 10= Burning Desire. DO NOT proceed until each of your teammates' score is at least an 8 thru 10.*
> ~Tom Peters

Take Action Now!
Step up your energy levels in everything you do! Don't ever let other people's draining energy pull you down. Be the positive force that unleashes the goodness in the world!

Recipes For Success Ingredient #54:
Your Master Mind

Your Greatness Is A Direct Reflection
Of The Quality Of Advisors In Your Life

Assemble Your Master Mind Alliance. No man is an island. We all stand on the shoulders of other people. Cultivate relationships with the best advisors who will support you and who will believe in you. This is one huge reason why you need to strive to be the best of the best in your craft. Your effort to master your craft will attract top experts who will be happy to mentor you as others have helped them earlier in their careers. Your involvement in your local Chamber of Commerce, Rotary Club, Lions Club, and other community organizations will put you in contact with the right people. These advisors may include: entrepreneurs, a good lawyer, financial advisors with proven track records, certified public accountants, investment bankers to help you raise money, and a public relations person who can help get you get free press to create the right public impression of your company. A Great Banker who can help you with your financing needs. A Computer Expert who can help you stay connected. A Great Insurance Agent who can help you through the complex world of insurance. And finally, a Friendly Clergyman… you will face tough times where it seems everything is caving in around you and you will definitely need help from a higher power. Never be embarrassed to pray during these tough times and always thank God for your blessings and abundance!

May the Force be with you!

~YODA, Jedi Master

Take Action Now!

Write down a list of the advisors that you need in your life to accomplish your life's greatest dreams. Throughout your life, you will have an opportunity to cultivate the right advisors, mentors, or coaches who can help provide guidance in putting together your own recipe for success!

Recipes For Success Ingredient #55:
Creating A Challenging Environment

Create A More Challenging
Environment Around You

The Only Goals Worth Achieving In Life Must Be So Big That They Transform You! Jim Rohn, America's Greatest Business Philosopher, said… "Don't go where it is easy, you won't grow. Go where it is hard." You must go where life challenges you. Every year, set higher goals. Take on a new job. Learn a new language. Teach. Write a book. Start a business. How can you make the world a better place? You can never become more than you are right now without going where you have never been before, doing the things you have never done before, and experiencing the things you have never experienced before! Once you reach your goals, start immediately to create a more challenging environment around you. Never get comfortable in one place. Most people live their lives recreating comfort zones of security… and they are miserable for good reason. Comfort Zones are Death Zones. Getting too comfortable is when you start to die and your physical and mental energy weakens. When you cease to learn, that is when you start dying. The quality of your life will always reflect how challenging your environment is!

In each of us are places where we have never gone. Only by pressing the limits do you ever find them.
~Dr. Joyce Brothers

Take Action Now!
Get ready to take on big challenges by starting small and changing things that you do daily that have become your comfort zone patterns. Change the route you take home. Explore different restaurants and order something you have never ordered before. Sit in a different chair at home! Get used to going outside your comfort zone. Next time a big opportunity comes along about which you have no clue over how you're going to make it happen… go ahead and seize your opportunities… you are ready to unleash your greatness!

Recipes For Success Ingredient #56:
Embrace Change

The Definition of INSANITY:
Doing The Same Thing Day In And Day Out
And Expecting Different Results!

Life Is About Change. The world is rapidly changing around you. Change is guaranteed. Change will happen whether you like it or not.... don't be a victim of change. Don't live a frustrated life trying to change the world. You can only change yourself. Become the master of change. Embrace change. Love Change! Transformation is good! The major key to change: Change does not happen "out in the world" ...real, lasting change only happens within you! Change your thinking... change your life. Once you change who you are... only then can you affect what happens around you through your example. More importantly, never underestimate the changes that YOU can make to transform the world!

Become the change that you want to see in the world.
~Mahatma Gandhi

Take Action Now!
I embrace change, I welcome change, I live for change... I can't wait to see the new me as I create new opportunities for success!

Recipes For Success Ingredient #57: Humility

Being Humble To Serve Takes Great Strength!

Be Humble. You unleash your greatness when you are able serve unselfishly. Being humble is actually a sign of great strength. The opposite of humbleness is arrogance. Arrogance is ignorance! There are times when you have to admit that you are your own worst enemy. You cannot change what you will not admit is wrong in your life. You cannot be of great service to others if you are full of yourself! I am reminded of a quote from a great world leader, Golda Meir... "Don't be humble. You're not that great!" You see... one of the greatest lessons in life is that ego and self-righteous pride are often our biggest stumbling blocks. Unfortunately, ego is supported by a strong case of denial. Only the strong are confident enough to be accepting of instruction. When you devote your life to the service of others... you need to be alert to the needs of others and you must give your undivided attention to listening to what they are telling you. You cannot do this when you are full of yourself. Humility is living your life in gratefulness.

Humility is the only true wisdom by Which we prepare our minds for all the possible changes of life.

~George Arliss

Take Action Now!

I will live my life in gratefulness. I will be alert and attentive to the needs of others. I will live my life striving to make the world a better place. I am unleashing my greatness by giving myself to the service of others.

Recipes For Success Ingredient #58:
Stepping Backwards to Go Forward

Sometimes It's Necessary To Take A Step Backwards
To Regroup To Move Forward Again

It's All About Moving Forward! There are times when you need to set your pride aside and take a few steps backwards, including taking a cut in pay, to move forward. Don't ever get caught in a comfort zone where you can't grow because you're afraid to start over! There will be times that you need to reinvent yourself. You need to have a flexible mindset. Be open to new ideas. Some times you need to learn new job skills that require you to start all over again. That's OK, just look at this time as an investment in your career. There have been times when I have seen someone get so angry when receiving a cut in pay to stay employed while a company was reorganizing that they quit while angry. Then they ended up having a heck of a time getting rehired. Then I have seen others who realized that their temporary setback was not personal. They regrouped, reinvented themselves, and it wasn't long before they were back on top again. You can always create new opportunities while you're employed, but it is very hard to get new jobs or find new opportunities while you are unemployed. Remember, it's all about moving forward... even if you do have to take a few steps back.

You are either growing or dying. There is no in between.
Even a farmer knows that after a harvest... the field must
be plowed under... in order to replant and start the
growing process all over again.
~Famous Dave Anderson

Take Action Now!
I will be aware that sometimes, to grow forward, I need to be flexible and unlearn so that I can be reborn into something new and amazing! Is there any area now that I need to relearn? How can I reinvent myself into something greater? I will take action now to transform myself and create new and better recipes for success!

Recipes For Success Ingredient #59:
When Life Is Not Fair

When Life Happens… I Will Step Up
And Happen To Life!

Life Is Unfair. This is just a fact of life! There will be times when you think you have been wronged and your first reaction will be to be blameful. NEVER BE BLAMEFUL… it serves no purpose. As hard as it is… don't let yourself be crippled by things that are unfair. You will find that there are people in your life that just don't like you… don't let these people get you down. They are not worth it. Suck it up! Get your positive attitude back and then use all of your energy to move forward with renewed hope for your future. When things get tough, stay focused on your dreams and your goals.

> *If life was fair, Elvis would be alive and all the impersonators would be dead!*
>
> ~Johnny Carson

Take Action Now!

I will be the life in life! I will never again let myself down because of events I can't control. I will step up and move forward, never looking back! I am ready to unleash my greatness and make this world a better place!!!

Recipes For Success Ingredient #60:
Only Speak Good Things

I Will Speak Goodness Into The World

Your Language Is Powerful... Don't Be A Whiner and A Complainer! Yes, life is difficult and that is why they call it life and not happy camp! When times get tough... everyone's first response is to whine and complain... but don't! It seems like the negative people are attracted to each other and then they wonder why they have all of the bad luck. I have found out the hard way that when I complain... everyone avoids me like the plague! Don't establish a reputation in your organization as a whiner and complainer. As an employer, believe me when I say... your supervisors know who the whiners and complainers are! Always be seen as cheerfully optimistic. When you are optimistic, no matter how difficult things may be... then the people who can help you... will come alongside you and support you. Your optimism during difficult times will attract better opportunities into your life.

> *People that pay for things never complain. It's the guy*
> *you give something to that you can't please.*
>
> ~Will Rogers

Take Action Now!

From this day forward, I refuse to mutter a whine, moan, or complaint. I will always be grateful. I will be forward looking. I will be optimistic looking forward into the future and believing that the best is yet to come!

Recipes For Success Ingredient #61:
Self Talk Your Way To Success

You Have The Power To Change Your Results
By Changing How You Talk

Your daily language determines your future. How you talk is critically important to your success. Have you ever listened to what comes out of your mouth? Many people would be shocked to hear how negative they talk throughout the day. They are full of excuses to justify why they didn't get something done. They are blameful of other people not wanting to take responsibility for the dismal lives they live. They have a ready ear for gossip or rumors and fill their heads with other people's trash. It seems like they thrive on any news of negative stuff happening on TV, the radio, or the newspapers. How do you talk? What do you listen to? What are you filling your head with? Your language is important to your success.

Positive self-talk is vital to programming your mind. You are in control of your destiny by what you allow to go into your mind. Why not take charge by consciously programming your mind with good things. Your mind listens to what you talk about. Only talk positive about other people. Look for the good in other people and share only these thoughts with whomever you are talking to. Tell yourself how wonderful you are. Pump yourself up when you are feeling down. Repeat your goals over again and again to yourself. From now on... no more negativity coming out of your mouth, no more garbage, no more gossip, and no more cuss words. Get rid of the "cant's" and the "try's". From now on... the only talk that is in your head or comes out of your mouth should be... "I can, I will, I am a winner, and I am Amazing; OR what you say to others... You can, You are, You are a Winner, and You are Amazing!"

The inner speech, your thoughts, can cause you to be rich or poor, loved or unloved, happy or unhappy, attractive or unattractive, powerful or weak.

~Ralph Charell

Take Action Now!

For one day catch every negative thing you say and write it down. Now consciously make sure everything you say from now on is only positive, uplifting, and edifying. Stop anyone wanting to tell you some juicy gossip. Turn off the TV or the radio when anything negative comes on. Don't read anything in the newspaper that's negative. Start filling your head with the pure, the good, and the powerful. Take control of your destiny by self-talking your way to success!

Recipes For Success Ingredient #62:
Be A Good Finder

I See Only The Goodness In Others

No Rumoring Or Gossiping! Human nature makes people interested in the problems of other people. The mind is precious and the Good Lord did not create your mind to be a garbage dump for other people's trash. When people come to you with a... "Did you hear...?" Tell them immediately that you're not interested in the adversities of other people... and that you're only interested if the purpose of the conversation will make a positive difference in somebody's life. When you genuinely care about people, you will want to help people. The energy that you put out into the Universe will always be multiplied and be returned back to you. What goes around... comes around.

Whoever gossips to you, will gossip about you!
~Sage Advice

Take Action Now!

I will look for only the best in others. I will be a good finder. I will be encouraging. The words I speak into the Universe will only be of positive energy.

Recipes For Success Ingredient #63:
Never Get Mad Again

Getting Mad Serves No Purpose

No More Getting Mad and Angry. This has been a problem for me but I have learned the hard way... there is no reason ever to lose your temper. When I look back... my anger never accomplished anything and it took away from my ability to create new opportunities going forward. You can accomplish a lot more if you stay collected and keep your wits about you. All you show is how immature you are when you lose your temper. When anger tempts you, ask yourself... "Am I moving forward?" Always be moving forward.

> *If a small thing has the power to get you angry, doesn't that indicate something about your size?*
>
> ~Sidney J. Harris

Take Action Now!

I vow to never get angry again. I will use this energy to make a positive difference in the lives of others. I will not bind up my precious mind with anger. Instead, I will create, I will dream, I will love, and I will give hope.

Recipes For Success Ingredient #64:
No Getting Even

I Will Live A Life Of Hope, Joy, and Love!

Revenge. Don't even go there… it is unproductive. Revenge like getting angry… serves no good purpose. As much as you feel you have the right to return the vengeance… don't! It never serves you. Always take the high road. Don't let the negative energy of someone else dictate your future. Let the Universe take care of your injustice. Live your life in love and you'll never have room for revenge. Never use your energy to crush the spirit of another person! The best advice that I have ever heard about "getting even" is to forgive!

> *Holding on to anger is like grasping a hot coal with the intent of throwing it at someone else… you are the one who gets burned.*
>
> ~Native American Wisdom

Take Action Now!

I will live my life in gratefulness no matter the injustice. I will rise above the hurt and I will forgive, forget, and move forward with a positive spirit! I will make the world a better place and I am moving closer to creating my own recipe for success!

Recipes For Success Ingredient #65:
Be Quick To Forgive

Forgiveness Is One Of Life's Greatest Virtues

Forgiveness Unleashes Our Greatness. We all make mistakes and sometimes we royally blow it... when this happens, we yearn for understanding, the opportunity to try again to make things right... and we all want forgiveness. All great people are quick to forgive. All little people dwell on how unfair life is and how they have been wronged. Don't bind up your mind with the grinding of revenge. Don't waste you positive energy living in the past. Don't dwell on things you can't change. Use your energy and your mind to move forward. The best thing you can do for yourself is to forgive. You cannot create new ideas and see new opportunities if you are bound up by resentment, anger, and blame. Remember this... if you don't forgive... you can never be forgiven! Forgive, Forget, and Move ON!

> *When you hold resentment toward another, you are bound to that person by an emotional link that is stronger than steel. Forgiveness is the only way to dissolve that link and get free.*
>
> ~Catherine Ponder

Take Action Now!

I will search my heart and completely and unconditionally forgive to all people... and I will begin my life anew. I will live my life in gratefulness. I will appreciate and love of all the people in the circle of my influence. I will make forgiveness one of my greatest character strengths.

Recipes For Success Ingredient #66:
Give Your Trust

Trust Is A Gift You Give and Receive

Trust People. You have to trust people to make things happen. Trusting people is the only way that they can experience how to be successful on their own. Be a believer in people… but also understand that part of the trust process is accountability. You need to "Inspect what you expect!" Only 3% of people will screw you… which means that 97% will do their best to support you. Don't live your life worried about the 3%. Focus on the 97% and build a thriving enterprise. The more you can trust other people… the greater the combined force you can put together to achieve greater accomplishments.

> *Few things can help an individual more than to place responsibility on him, and let him know that you trust him.*
>
> ~Booker T. Washington

Take Action Now!

I will live my life in trust. I will believe in people… and I will live my life worthy of other people's trust.

Recipes For Success Ingredient #67:
Organize Your Life

Organization Frees You To Succeed

Be Organized and Clean. There is absolutely no way you can be successful without being totally organized. I have no problem telling you that this is one of my personal greatest weaknesses, as I have Adult Attention Deficit Disorder. Knowing this, I have learned how to surround myself with people who keep me organized. I do not tolerate disorganization from others! Everything must be kept clean and organized. I have often said... If I could re-educate myself... I would join the military just to go through boot camp! The discipline and organization that you learn in the military is invaluable to a person's success in life. Keep yourself organized at home and at your place of business. Make organization, neatness, and cleanliness... your greatest character strengths.

> *The things I learned in the Marine Corps have stayed with me to this day. I hate being late. I'm very organized, and I'm not afraid to take responsibility for my own actions.*
>
> ~Drew Carey

Take Action Now!

From this day forward, I will live an organized life. Organization will free me to unleash my greatness!

Recipes For Success Ingredient #68:
Be The Best Of The Best

I Live To Give My Best To Others

Create Your "Best Of The Best List." Everyone is taught to write down their dreams and turn them into goals. Here's another great idea... Create a "Best List" of everything associated with your life and your career. When I started Famous Dave's... I made a list of almost 100 items that I would be the best at. I was going to have: The Best Ribs, The Best Barbeque Sauce, The Best Cole Slaw, The Best Take Out Menu, The Best Training Program, etc, etc. And today, we have won more Best Of Class recognitions than any restaurant in history! Over 400 First Place Awards at the time of this writing. Make a list that identifies everything that you can be the absolute best at! Make an unbreakable promise to yourself to give 100% of your total effort to strive for excellence in whatever you do... so that you can be The Best of The Best!... not to call attention to yourself... but because your customers deserve only your best! Keep this list someplace where you can see it every day.

> *If you want to achieve excellence, you can get there today. As of this second, quit doing less-than-excellent work.*
>
> ~Thomas J. Watson

Take Action Now!

I will identify things that I give to my customers, my family, and my friends and I will make sure that I am giving my absolute best! I give my best because my loved ones, my friends, and my customers deserve nothing but my best! Giving your best to the world is the quickest way to unleashing your greatness!

Recipes For Success Ingredient #69:
The Profit Principle

Profit Is Creating Added Value In
The Lives Of Other People

Know How To Create Profits. Profit is not what I get but how I create added value in the lives of other people. Most people live their lives thinking that they need "to get" ...The Profit Principle is all about first giving your best to others. Profit is simply creating "Added Value" in the lives of others. Profit is enlargement. Profit is giving more than what is expected. Profit is creating increase... increase in added value... increase in added productivity. Profit is making the world a better place. Live your life in "Profit Awareness"... profit awareness is living your life where your every moment is driven to consistently give more than is expected and leaving the world a better place because of your influence, hard work, and your generosity. When you give more than is expected, you unleash great energy into the Universe, and this creates a multiplier effect that will return unlimited wealth and unlimited opportunities for you!

> *My father once told me...that anyone who worked for three dollars an hour... owed to himself to put in four dollars' worth of work.*
>
> ~Bill Russell

Take Action Now!

I will live my life creating added value in the lives of other people. I will give more than is expected. I will leave this world a better place and unleash my greatness by adding value to everything in my influence!

Recipes For Success Ingredient #70:
Financial Literacy

Money Is A Measurement Of My Unselfish Giving
To Make The World A Better Place

Understand The Dynamics Of Money. Money is Energy! Become Financially Literate. If you have never studied wealth... it's a good reason why you struggle with your finances. Never come from a mindset that money is lacking in your life. When you live your life in the service of others, you will attract all of the abundance that you need to accomplish all of your wildest dreams! There is no limit to abundance. When you learn how to serve and make others happy... wealth is basically unlimited! When you only think about satisfying yourself... then wealth becomes hard to find. Unleash the abundance of the universe by helping others first. Always remember this... wealth does not come from what you earn... wealth only comes from your ability to create your own investment portfolio. Robert Kiyosaki's *Rich Dad Poor Dad* is a good book for starting your Financial Success Library.

> *One of the reasons the rich get richer, the poor get poorer and the middle class struggles in debt is because the subject of money is taught at home, not at school.*
> ~Robert Kiyosaki

Take Action Now!
I will take steps to become financially literate. There is no limit to my earning ability when I give unselfishly of everything I have: my ideas, my energy, my work, my love, to the betterment of other people. When I give my all to make the world a better place, I am providing the right ingredients for not only my success but the success of everyone in my influence!

Recipes For Success Ingredient #71:
Create More ~ Consume Less

Create More Than You Consume
And You'll Never Be Without!

In Everything You Do, Ask Yourself... "Am I Creating Or Consuming? ...If I Am Consuming... How Am I Going To Create Something Of Greater Value? Every day, every waking moment, you should consciously be figuring out how to create something of more value than what you are consuming. This is one of the simple secrets to unlimited success. Consuming without producing is living your life in the negative. Always give more value than what you are paid, and you will be paid more. When you are creating, you are tapping into the Universe's unlimited resources. Whatever you touch should be left better not depleted. The Wisdom of the Universe says to create more and produce more than what was expected and you will be swamped with abundance. When you figure out how to always create more value and give more than what was expected... then the world will seek you out with unlimited opportunity!

> *You don't get paid for the hour. You get paid for the value you bring to the hour!*
>
> ~Jim Rohn

Take Action Now!
From this day forward, I will live my life consciously creating more than I consume. As my needs increase, I will be more productive. As I learn how to create more than I consume, I will be moving closer to unleashing my greatness!

Recipes For Success Ingredient #72:
Be Alert At Work

I Will Be Thoroughly Knowledgeable
And Aware About My Business

Know Your Business. Be aware of everything that goes on at work. This is not "being nosey" …this all about being alert. Every business has a "Right Way" of doing things. Most businesses have policy and procedure manuals but 99% of the employees never know what's in them. Become the expert. Become the master of your company's information. Be able to tear things apart and put them back together again. Here's an important point: "Know where things can fall through the cracks!" Be the one everyone goes to… for answers. When you love what you are doing, you will know everything there is to know about your business. Don't ever let another competitor know more about your business or your industry than you… and if they do… you better study what they are doing and learn from them! Most of all… keep everyone informed. Make NO SURPRISES your motto!

If you want to be successful, it's just this simple: Know what you are doing. Love what you are doing. And believe in what you are doing.

~Will Rogers

Take Action Now!

I will master my business. I will take nothing for granted. I will not assume anything I will be attentive, alert, and observant. I will take great notes so that I will never forget important things about my work.

Recipes For Success Ingredient #73:
Be A Builder of People

I Grow By Helping People Grow

Be A Builder of People. No man is an island. You cannot be successful without people. See the best in people. Encourage others to strive to reach their potential. Believe in people. They will fail just as you will fail… this is when you need to see past their failures and you need to become stronger to lift them up. Tom Peters, one of America's best business consultants, said, "How do you humiliate and demean someone and then expect him or her to care about product quality?" Never use your energy to crush the spirit of another person. Praise people and they will flourish. Never see people as they are… see people as they could be. Give hope.

Catch your peers doing something right. When you enter your place of work, you never leave it at zero. You either make it a little better or a little worse. Make it a little better.

~Marcus Buckingham

Take Action Now!

I will inspire, educate, and coach the people within my influence to reach higher levels of success and achievement. I will be quick to acknowledge other people's talents and accomplishments, and praise them for their contributions. I will be a raving ambassador for the people on my team. By helping other people grow into their greatness, I am creating the best recipe for success possible!

Recipes For Success Ingredient #74:
Teaching Is A Gift

Teaching Unleashes The Greatness In Others

Be A Teacher. All great people teach. We all had a favorite teacher who inspired us and opened our minds to what is possible. The greatest gift you can give another person is hope. When you can teach a person how to unleash the talent and giftedness each person has within them... you bring goodness to the entire universe. Freely share your knowledge and hold nothing back. Help someone become better. When you can share your knowledge, you become better at what you do. There is magical, multiplying goodness from teaching. You can really jumpstart your career by being able to teach others what you know! The old philosophy of job security was to protect your knowledge and then people would think you were valuable... the truth is that this type of thinking caused more business failures. The right philosophy is to strive to become the best you can be for the sole purpose of being able to teach others the best practices, the right way to get things done, and how they can succeed. The Universe favors those who teach!

> *You can't love what you don't know much about. You can't convince, stimulate, hold the attention, teach, if you don't know what you're talking about!*
> ~David McCullough

Take Action Now!
I will seize every opportunity to teach those in my influence. I will inspire, give hope, and expand their horizons of greatness. The more I teach and grow other people, the more I expand my own opportunities for greatness!

Recipes For Success Ingredient #75: Empowerment

Empowering Others For Success
Unleashes Your Greatness

Multiply Your Efforts Through The Masses. One of the Major Keys to great success is being able to influence the masses. This will only happen when you are obsessively devoted to the betterment of others. Live your life to empower those in your influence. Trust them. Give them opportunity. Learn how to multiply your ability to maximize your unlimited potential by providing your product or services to the masses. Learn how to unleash other people to accomplish your dreams or provide your services to the masses. You cannot achieve great success without reaching the masses… and you cannot reach the masses without being a positive influence on the masses.

> *Your enthusiastic love for what you are doing will attract other people who share the same level of passion. When this happens you create an unstoppable force that can accomplish great things overcoming all obstacles especially if your collective goals are to make this world a better place.*
>
> ~Famous Dave Anderson

Take Action Now!

I will unleash my own greatness and my contribution to the world by empowering the people within my influence. I will teach them how to live their lives in service to others. I will freely share my knowledge, wisdom, ideas, and my energy to inspire, motivate, encourage, and teach.

Recipes For Success Ingredient #76:
Greatness Through Adversity

I Will Learn How To Become
My Ultimate Best Through Adversity

Adversity Is Almost Guaranteed. Don't fear tough times. You will encounter unbelievable adversity, tough challenges, and complete failure in your life. That is OK... this is how you learn. This is how your character gets defined. Don't give up on yourself... you will get through your tough times. Learn how to turn your adversities and failures into unlimited successes. Learn how to turn your weaknesses into your greatest opportunities. The greater your success, the greater your exposure to life's tough problems. Sometimes it seems like you are the only one that life has singled out to receive more than your fair share of problems. Just remember this... all great people and great leaders, and all successful people have had incredibly tough times in their lives, just like you... but they never gave up! All achievers in life resolve with unwavering determination that they will not let life's challenges weaken them but that they will get stronger because of them. People of influence admire and respect people who never give up under life's tough challenges.

> *Obstacles cannot crush me. Every obstacle yields to stern resolve. He who is fixed on a star does not change his mind.*
>
> ~Leonardo Da Vinci

Take Action Now!

I will not fear adversity. I will not beat myself up over failure. I will stay positive and optimistic. I will survive. I will overcome. I will be better prepared to take on even greater opportunities because of what I have learned through my adversities! I am a winner! I am a Superstar! I am moving closer to my greatness through adversity!!!

Recipes For Success Ingredient #77:
Life Is Not Fair

It's A Good Thing Life Is Not Fair!

Life Happens. No matter how much of a good person you may think you are… there are times when life is not fair and there isn't a damn thing you can do about it! If you find things aren't going your way… maybe there's a reason why. You need to learn how to "roll with the punches… in boxing, you are taught how to "roll with the punches" instead of taking a hit full force. The strongest trees bend. Pure gold is malleable while gold with impurities is brittle. A river is a powerful force as it slowly, over time, wears out its obstacles. In the face of adversity, stay the course. You will find out that none of us are really in control as much as we would like to think. If you want to make God laugh… "Tell him your plans!"

> *If all things happened fairly… I would never have had the incredible opportunities I have experienced. Sometimes it is better to be disadvantaged because you have to challenge yourself!*
>
> ~Famous Dave Anderson

Take Action Now!

I will make the most out of every moment. I will not take things so seriously. Living my life in gratefulness will allow me to be at peace with myself when things don't go my way. I will be accepting of these things and I will move on. I will always keep moving forward.

Recipes For Success Ingredient #78:
Learn Through Mistakes

You're A Success If The Mistakes
You Make Are New Ones!

Mistakes Will Happen. Mistakes and failures are all part of life and they are important learning lessons in your journey of success. Make sure you learn something. When you learn from your mistakes... they go from being "mistakes" and are turned into your "education." Sometimes your education is expensive! When you fail... don't hesitate to confess. Ask for forgiveness and do whatever is necessary to make things right. Always be up front about what happened. Never let people become surprised by your mistake or failure. Most importantly, don't let your mind become preoccupied with something that has already happened and you can't do anything about it. Don't let your mind become filled with blamefulness. You must fill your mind and your spirit with optimism about creating new opportunities, a new future, a new beginning... and moving forward.

> *Would you like me to give you a formula for success? It's quite simple, really. Double your rate of failure! You're thinking of failure as the enemy of success. But it isn't at all... You can be discouraged by failure or can learn from it.*
>
> ~Thomas J. Watson

Take Action Now!

Mistakes are my opportunity to grow. From this day forward... I will be open about the mistakes and failures in my life and I will use these opportunities to keep growing.

Recipes For Success Ingredient #79:
Never Quit

You Can't Stop A Man Who Won't Quit!

When Everything Seems Hopeless And You Are About To Quit—Don't... You Are Closer To Success Than You Think! When you are striving to achieve higher levels of accomplishment and you are out on the edge... there will be unexpected adversities that will rip you apart. You will feel abandoned and you will want to scream out to the Universe to give you a break. The greater your success... the greater your risk of failure. Just remember this... you cannot be enormously successful being the person you are right now. The thinking and behavior that got you to where you are today are not the thinking and behavior that you need to stretch to where you want to grow tomorrow. The struggle grows you and transforms you... and this is good! The Universe only rewards your greatest dreams when you dig down deep to keep trying. When you make up your mind that you are never going to give up—that's when the Universe knows you are ready for greatness... and it's then... that the Universe will release the floodgates of abundance. Don't ever give up. Especially... don't ever give up on your dreams!

The temptation to quit will be the greatest just before you are about breakthrough to success!
~The Wisdom of The Universe

Take Action Now!

I start what I begin. I am not a quitter! I will make it through this day. I will not quit. I am tough. I am a Winner. I am a Champion. I am a Superstar. When I make up my mind to give everything, my all, I am Unleashing My Greatness!

Recipes For Success Ingredient #80:
Be Optimistic

Things Always Work Out

Cultivate Optimism In Your Life. There's a difference between being "positively happy" and being optimistic. Optimistic is not happy camp. You can be positively happy and yet frozen in front of a mountain of obstacles that render you delusional and ineffective. Being "optimistic" is knowing that "there is" a mountain of obstacles before you but you believe that somehow, someway... you are going to go over, go around, or go through your obstacles because you are determined to never give up. A positive mindset that is resolved to never give up will overcome the most devastating failures. Be Persistent. Be Relentless. The greater the opportunity... the greater your risk. Risk will create times where you want to give up... you must think... giving up is never an option. A positive "forward" attitude, strong work ethic, a willingness to give more than expected... all lived with total all-out energy... will yield results beyond your wildest expectations!

> *Success is to be measured not so much by the position that one has reached in life as by the obstacles which he has overcome.*
>
> ~Booker T. Washington

Take Action Now!

I will live my life being "Solution Conscious not Problem Conscious." I will believe that things will always work out... believing that The Best Is Yet To Come! When I am determined to never give up... I am creating the best opportunities for success!

Recipes For Success Ingredient #81:
Enjoy Yourself

Don't Take Yourself Too Seriously!

Have Fun! Some people wonder why I work all the time... I am having fun. If you love what you are doing... you'll never work another day again in your life! I love writing, I love swimming, and I love cooking great-tasting food for guests of Famous Dave's. That's the one thing I love about Famous Dave's... we have a great group of team members that love having a good time feeding great barbeque to our raving, loyal fans. Yes, sometimes I get deep into my work but that's when I appreciate my wife who always has a ready laugh. I enjoy watching my grandkids laugh and play. I have several friends who are great laughers and I keep these friends around me. Keep a ready smile on your face. Brighten up every room you walk into with energy! Be quick to laugh. Don't take things so seriously. Have fun!

Just Play. Have Fun. Enjoy The Game.
~Michael Jordan

Take Action Now!
I will find something to laugh at every day. I will laugh out loud. I may even laugh at you!

Recipes For Success Ingredient #82:
Trust Yourself

Your Intuition Is God's Way Of Connecting You
To The Wisdom Of The Universe

Trust Your Intuition. There are times when you just have to trust your "gut feel" …this is called intuition. This is your sixth sense. It is the wisdom of God's great universe connecting with you. Honor your intuition. Trust yourself. Most people second guess themselves and listen to others. Turn this around… start second-guessing others and start trusting your own intuition. In my own life… I have had second guesses where I wished I had listened to my own heart instead of following the advice of others… and, as a result, I have had some pretty awful, huge failures. Keep your own counsel. God has blessed you with a very remarkable mind… trust it! When you are getting "a feeling" …don't second-guess this divine connection… go with what's in your heart.

No matter how deep a study you make… what you really have to rely on is your own intuition and when it comes right down to it, you really don't know what's going to happen until you do it.

~Konosuke Matsushita

Take Action Now!

From this day forward… I will trust my own intuition… and second-guess what other people are saying! I will honor what my heart is telling me. God has given me an incredible mind and an amazing spirit… I will trust my own intuition. When I follow my dreams, I am honoring the spirit I have been blessed with by an Almighty Living God! I am blessed. I am amazing. I am incredible. I am designed for accomplishment and greatness!

Recipes For Success Ingredient #83:
I Will Give Thanks

Living In Gratefulness
Empowers Your Spirituality

Live Your Life In Gratitude. Be thankful for everything you have and you will never live a life in frustration, wanting things that are out of your reach. The Wisdom of The Universe says, "Gratefulness and appreciation create a spiritual aura around you that attracts more blessings." Don't ever be ashamed to stop and give thanks to your creator for all that you have been blessed with! There are healing powers in being grateful. Finding little things to be thankful for will attract greater blessings and abundance in your life. Today, I tell everyone that I live every day of my life in gratitude and it's not because of the success of Famous Dave's, although I am very grateful for how my passion has evolved into a very successful restaurant company. But here's the real reason why I am grateful... I should have been dead three times... and today I know that God has a higher purpose for me on this planet... and that's to make a positive difference in the lives of others. I am grateful for my family. I am grateful for my health. And I am grateful for my friends. Above all, I am grateful that we live in such a great country where we can all achieve our dreams.

I have found that when I am grateful for the love of family and friends... it somehow allows me to experience the love they have in their hearts...their love belongs to me. When you are grateful, you attract what is the best in others back into your life. Live your life in gratefulness and you will never be wanting...you will live your life in richness!

~Famous Dave Anderson

Take Action Now!
I will live my life in gratefulness. Sincere thankfulness unleashes unlimited abundance into my life.

Recipes For Success Ingredient #84:
Your Community Spirit

Live To Make The World A Better Place

Develop A Strong, Unselfish Community Spirit. We all live so that our children have better opportunities than us. It has been said... it takes a village to grow a child. I always want to hire people who are active in their communities. I found it interesting to talk with a high level executive who was transferring to a new territory about what he looked for when relocating to a new community. He said, "I look for a good school system... not for the good school system... but for the community that values and invests in their school system!" You cannot be apathetic in thinking that it's OK to leave the affairs of your community up to "other" people. Everyone must get involved with creating a strong community. Everyone's ideas and opinions are needed. Strong communities are needed for businesses to thrive and create good paying job opportunities. Strong communities are needed for good "up-to-date, relevant schools" to provide a great education for our youth and communities where our children can play safely without fear. Our children will grow into tomorrow's leaders representing high values and integrity. And these children will grow into the ideal employee candidates with great work ethic. Get involved with developing the youth in your community. Finally, strong communities are needed to provide places where people are free to worship.

> *Volunteering is the ultimate exercise in democracy. You vote in elections once a year, but when you volunteer, you vote every day about the kind of community you want to live in.*
>
> ~Marjorie Moore

Take Action Now!

I will go to school board meetings. I will join my local Chamber of Commerce. I will vote. I will be more involved in my community. I am unleashing my greatness by helping to build a strong community.

Recipes For Success Ingredient #85:
Generosity

Sincere Unselfish Giving Unleashes
The Universe's Abundance!

Give Until It Feels Good! Give generously of your time, your ideas, your hard work, and your finances to your community. The bigger the window that you give out of… the more that can be shoved back to you! Be generous. If you don't give… you are clogging up the pipes. Givers Win… Takers Lose. Sir Winston Churchill, one of the world's greatest leaders, once said… "You make a living by what you earn; you make a life by what you give."

> *You give but little when you give of your possessions. It*
> *is when you give of yourself that you truly give.*
>
> ~Kahlil Gibran

Take Action Now!

I will live a life in the service of others. I am creating the best recipe for success by giving all of my best to make this world a better place!

THE BUILDER

I saw a gang of men from my home town
A gang of men tearing a building down,
With a heave and a ho and a yes yes yell,
they swung a beam and a sidewall fell.

And I went up to the foreman and said, "Are these men skilled?
Like the ones you'd use if you had to build?"
And he laughed and said, "Oh no, no indeed,
the most common labor is all I need...
for I can destroy in a day...
what has taken a builder ten years to build."

So I thought to myself as I went on my way...
Which one of these roles am I willing to play?
Am I one who is tearing down as I carelessly make my way around?

Or am I one whose community will be a little bit better... just because I
was there?

- Author Unknown

Have Famous Dave Anderson Speak to Your Audience!

A highly sought after keynote speaker, Famous Dave holds nothing back as he shares his incredible real life story of overcoming tremendous odds, adversity, and failure to create one of America's best loved restaurant companies. With passion, energy, and enthusiasm...Dave shares how he overcame his own personal challenges to become America's Rib King...he connects directly to the spirit of every heart in attendance. Dave Anderson is an Inspiring Speaker and Successful Entrepreneur whose "Against All Odds" story is living proof that the American Dream... no longer has to be just a dream!

Famous Dave Anderson's most requested keynotes include:

- **Entrepreneurship:** The Famous Dave's Story...How I Took a Backyard Hobby and Turned it Into a $500 Million Restaurant Empire!

- **Against All Odds**: How to Overcome Life's Adversities and Turn Them Into Your Greatest Opportunities!

- **The Accelerated Changing Marketplace**: Don't Be a Victim of Change... Become the Architect of Your Own Destiny!

- **Sobriety, Freedom, and A New Life**: A Faith Based Message of Hope and Deliverance From Addictions

In addition to his highly-motivating and dynamic keynote presentations, Famous Dave Anderson provides...

- Corporate Coaching for Business Success & Marketing

- Branding Evaluations and Coaching for Businesses

To Request Dave as a Keynote Speaker or learn more about his personalized coaching programs for businesses please contact Dave through his website, www.FamousDaveAnderson.com

Did you enjoy the book and want to Learn More? Add these great Famous Dave Anderson Books & CDs to your Success Library today!

Famous Dave Anderson's LifeSkills for Success: *The Ultimate Manual for Success and Achievement*

Famous Dave Anderson's Award Winning Backroads & Sidestreets Barbeque Grill Cookbook...*all my award winning recipes. A must for any serious cook or barbeque fanatic!*

Famous Dave Anderson & James Anderson's Report Cards to Paychecks: *How to Succeed in College and Land the Job of Your Dreams (coming soon)*

Famous Dave Anderson's The Entrepreneur's Bootcamp: *Famous Dave Anderson Reveals the Inside Secrets to How He Took a Backyard Hobby and Turned it into a $500 Million a Year Restaurant Empire. Street-Smart Strategies for Business Success and Your Career! (coming soon)*

Famous Dave Anderson's Personal Message of Sobriety: *A Heartfelt Story of Overcoming Addiction and Living a Life of Gratitude*

Famous Dave Anderson's Hog Heaven University: *Famous Dave Spills the Beans and Reveals All his Award Winning Secrets to Great Barbequing!*

Famous Dave Anderson's BBQ Pitmaster Secrets Revealed DVD: *A great how-to video that details all the secrets to a really great barbeque. A must for every barbeque fanatic!*

Have James Speak to Your Audience!

INSPIRING   MOTIVATING   CHALLENGING

James W. Anderson is America's Success Speaker!
To book James for your next conference or event, please contact:
James Anderson Productions

Office: 952.929.1678 or

info@jamesandersonproductions.com

We want to hear from you!

Log onto www.jamesandersonproductions.com and leave me
feedback on how this book has inspired you, and receive a
FREE MP3 Download of success tips!

Leaders Listen to James!

" After 25 years of listening and learning about
personal development, I believed I had learned
"it all".   I was mistaken, I learned new things
because of James about becoming a **better**
manager, father and individual. James brought
the message home with passion and conviction,
James was insightful and convincing, I was
moved to see such wisdom in a young man. I
have a lot of appreciation to James for helping
me take a few more steps up the personal
development ladder. "

- Gary Chappell, President/CEO,
Nightingale Conant

*Read James W. Anderson's latest books, Yesterday's Wisdom, Today's
Success, Great Results Start With Great Thoughts for Teens, and
Report Cards to Paychecks.*

www.FamousDaveAnderson.com

Famous Dave Anderson Proudly Presents:
The LifeSkills Executive Leadership Bootcamp

Get ready to jumpstart your life and experience in one of most impactful, life transforming leadership trainings in America! Stand Up and Stand Out from the masses. Gain an unfair advantage over everyone else by taking this incredible two-day, Executive Leadership Bootcamp. I have spent over two decades researching the top training programs in the world and personally spent over $2 Million dollars creating one of the most effective top level training programs available today. You owe it to yourself and your career to gain the leadership skills needed to compete in today's challenging marketplace.

My life and level of success completely changed after I went through a rigorous leadership training program in the early 1970's. It transformed how I thought, how I acted, and how I went after my goals, hopes and dreams. In fact, I believe that all my success is a direct result of this training experience. And because of that experience, it became my goal to create one of the best Leadership Training programs that would help me launch Famous Dave's of America. The results at Famous Dave's has been spectacular! And now you have a rare opportunity to experience for yourself... the most results-driven, powerful, challenging, and inspiring leadership intensive experiences you will ever experience. This course is designed to challenge you out of your comfort zones and get you set up for a life of uncommon success and achievement.

"I have worked in the personal and professional development industry for **over 25 years**. I attended the LifeSkills training and out of dozens I have attended, LifeSkills is the **most rewarding and beneficial training I have ever experienced.**"
– Gary Chappell, CEO, Nightingale-Conant, The World's Largest Personal Development Training Company

"This unique training experience has energized our Executive Committee and we have brought this energy back to the hotel and incorporated our new found skills into our daily business and personal lives. This has been a learning, personal growth, and life changing event. I would highly recommend LifeSkills trainings for all Executive Committee's for any organization."

Hilton Minneapolis Executive Team

- John Luke, GM, Hilton Minneapolis

"The results of this program are unbelievable and almost immeasurable. This course isn't about teaching, it is about transformation! You will become a better person, personally and professionally."

– Bill Morrissey, Founder & CEO, Morrissey Hospitality Companies (Mgt company for the Saint Paul Hotel – named one of the world's TOP 100 Hotels)

We have had the honor of having some of the most successful people, businesses and companies represented in our trainings....**Let us share how we can help energize you or your team to greater achievement and success.**

To Learn More About the
LifeSkills Trainings & Workshops Visit:

www.LifeskillsBusiness.com
